Marijuana Mastery

Essential Strategies for a Successful Grow

Tyler Harris

Table of Contents

INTRODUCTION

Welcome to "Marijuana Mastery: Essential Strategies for a Successful Grow." Unlike other sources, this in-depth book is designed to equip you with the fundamental knowledge and techniques required to grow superior marijuana plants, regardless of your level of experience or your aspiration to start your first cannabis-growing endeavor.

Growing marijuana has changed over the past few years from being a specialized pastime to a complex and sophisticated industry. More people are becoming interested in the fascinating realm of home cultivation as legalization grows and public perceptions change. But as interest in this area grows, so does the demand for precise, helpful, and thorough instruction.

This e-book is your guide to becoming an expert in the art and science of marijuana cultivation. Every facet of the growing process will be covered, from choosing the best strain for your particular requirements to figuring out the nuances of various growth stages. Every chapter is designed to give you practical methods, tried-and-true approaches, and insightful information to put you on the road to success.

We'll explore the basic principles of cannabis plants, taking you through their anatomy, life cycle, and many cultivars. You'll discover how to set up the best possible growth conditions, both inside and outside, and how vital lighting, ventilation, and equipment are to your plants' general health and yield.

We stress a comprehensive approach to marijuana growth throughout the e-book, combining morally and environmentally sound methods. We'll review everything you need to know to optimize your yields, potency, and general success—from germination to harvest.

"Marijuana Mastery" is your ultimate guide whether you're growing for personal use or considering a more ambitious project. Our goal is to equip you with the keys to successful marijuana cultivation and guide you toward mastery beyond gardening. Together, let's sow knowledge, foster growth, and reap success.

CHAPTER I

Understanding Cannabis Plants

Anatomy and Lifecycle

The cornerstone of a successful marijuana grow is derived from an awareness of the anatomy and lifespan of cannabis plants, which provide growers with a thorough understanding of the structure and developmental stages of the plant. Being a dioecious plant, cannabis possesses both male and female reproductive organs, each of which plays a unique role in the process of propagation. The roots, stems, leaves, flowers, and seeds are the distinct elements that make up a cannabis plant's anatomy.

For stability and nutrition absorption, the root system is essential. A robust root system guarantees the plant gets the water and minerals it needs, encouraging general growth. In addition to offering structural support, the stem facilitates the movement of carbohydrates, nutrients, and water throughout the plant. Nodes, which are vital locations where branches and leaves arise and contain the potential for future growth, are found in the stem.

The central locations for photosynthesis, the leaves, are crucial in transforming light energy into necessary carbohydrates. The cannabis plant is easily recognized by its unique fan-shaped leaves, which also indicate the plant's general health. Buds, or cannabis flowers, are the reproductive structures of the plant that hold the cannabinoids that provide the plant its therapeutic and intoxicating properties.

Growers looking to maximize productivity and potency must comprehend the cannabis lifecycle. Three main stages make up the lifecycle: germination, vegetative growth, and blooming.

The cannabis plant begins to live when it germinates. In this phase, water is absorbed by the seed, which starts the enzymatic reactions that convert stored energy into plant growth. The emerging seedling's cotyledons, or initial leaves, unfold to initiate photosynthesis. The ideal environmental conditions must be provided to encourage strong germination, including enough moisture, warmth, and light.

The plant moves into the vegetative growth stage after germination, which is marked by rapid growth and development. The plant concentrates on growing a solid structure, making leaves, and creating a robust root system at this stage. Vegetative development is promoted by tampering with the light cycle, usually by implementing an 18-6 or 24-0 light-dark cycle (18 hours of light, 6 hours of darkness, or continuous light). Pruning and training are two methods that cultivators can use to shape plants and maximize light exposure for higher yield.

The crucial time the plant turns its attention from growth to reproduction is during the flowering stage. Changes in light cycles cause the shift, and most farmers mimic natural circumstances by using a 12–12 light–dark cycle (12 hours of light, 12 hours of darkness). Male plants generate pollen for fertilization, while female plants develop buds with trichomes—resinous structures rich in cannabinoids. Male plants must be quickly identified and removed to avoid unintentional pollination, which could impair the quality of the female flowers.

Cultivators need to comprehend the subtleties of each stage if they are to adjust their methods to the plant's unique requirements at various stages of its lifetime. Creating ideal growing conditions at every stage is essential to successful cultivation because it builds a strong base for robust plants and abundant harvests.

A deep understanding of the subtle differences between various cannabis strains is also necessary for optimal production, in addition to knowledge of their basic anatomy and lifecycle. The cannabis genus is diverse, allowing for a wide range of strains with different traits, such as growth patterns, THC levels, and flavors. When choosing a strain for cultivation, it's essential to consider the intended effects, the amount of space available, and the surrounding conditions.

The two main varieties of cannabis are Indica and sativa, each with its unique qualities. Since Indica strains are frequently linked to drowsiness and relaxation, they are well-liked options for use in the evening or at night. Due to their bushier and lower stature, these plants are suitable for indoor growing when vertical space is limited. However, sativa strains are recognized for their stimulating and elevating qualities, which makes them perfect for daytime consumption. Taller and more slender growth patterns are characteristic of Sativa plants, which makes them ideal for outdoor production where vertical space is less restricted.

Blending the most significant traits from both indica and sativa genomes, hybrid strains provide a middle ground. Hybrids can be cultivated to produce various flavors and effects, satisfying a more comprehensive range of consumer preferences. Another essential factor to consider when choosing a strain is its cannabinoid concentration. The two most well-known cannabinoids, tetrahydrocannabinol (THC) and cannabinoid (CBD), each have unique effects. THC causes the psychoactive "high" that comes with cannabis, but CBD has medicinal advantages without the euphoric effects. Growers can accommodate the needs of both recreational and medical users using strains that have different ratios of THC to CBD.

Each strain has a distinct flavor profile and terpene concentration, adding to its individuality. Cannabis contains fragrant molecules called terpenes that affect the plant's flavor and aroma. Growers who are looking to produce cannabis with specific tastes or scents might look into strains that have different terpene profiles, which can range from earthy and flowery to citrusy and fruity.

In summary, understanding the structure and life cycle of cannabis plants is essential for any grower hoping to succeed in the marijuana industry. A comprehensive grasp of the nuances of root development and the dynamic stages of germination, vegetative growth, and blooming is essential for making well-informed decisions at every stage of the cultivation process. Choosing the correct strain adds another complexity, forcing growers to consider how genetics, effects, and flavors interact. With this thorough understanding, growers may successfully traverse the complex world of marijuana growth and eventually become experts in the art and science of producing this adaptable plant.

Differentiating Between Cannabis Varieties

Understanding the broad spectrum of cannabis strains and their distinctive qualities is necessary for marijuana growing, and it also requires differentiating between cannabis kinds. Cannabis is a very adaptable plant with many growth patterns, tastes, effects, and cannabinoid levels. The plant's diverse genetic makeup, which results in innumerable hybrid strains containing different mixtures of indica, sativa, and ruderalis traits, is partly responsible for this diversity. The two main subspecies of cannabis, indica, and sativa, each provide unique characteristics to the range of cannabis variations.

Indian subcontinent-originating Indica strains are frequently linked to calming and soothing effects. Due to their shorter stature and more compact nature, these plants are excellent choices for indoor growing where space may be at a premium. Because indices produce a body-centered "stoned" feeling, they are often used in the evening or at night. Compared to Sativa strains, Indica plants often blossom for a shorter time and have larger, darker leaves.

Conversely, sativa strains from tropical areas are prized for their stimulating and elevating qualities. Due to their more slender and taller growth patterns, sativas thrive well outdoors where vertical space is less of a constraint. Because sativa plants are acclimated to warmer climates than indica plants, their leaves are narrower and lighter in color. Since sativa strains promote creativity and attention without having the sleepy effects of Indica strains, they are frequently preferred for daytime use.

Indica and Sativa genetics have been crossed to create hybrid strains, which combine the finest traits of each subspecies to develop a medium ground. Breeders can produce various strains with different flavors, effects, and growth patterns through hybridization. Hybridization aims to create plants that serve a more comprehensive range of customer tastes by combining the energizing impact of sativas with the calming effects of indicas to provide a personalized experience.

The differences between indica and sativa go beyond just their effects; they also include the traits of the plants and the conditions under which they are cultivated. Because of their compact form, Indica plants grow best inside, where farmers can control the atmosphere to optimize production. Due to their larger size and extended flowering times, sativa plants do best outdoors with lots of sunshine and room to grow.

Although the classifications of indica and sativa offer a wide range of possibilities, the contemporary cannabis industry recognizes the limitations of this dichotomous framework. To properly distinguish between types, many growers and consumers understand the importance of considering additional criteria like THC concentration and terpene profiles.

The chemical substances that cannabis plants produce, called cannabinoids, are essential in determining the effects of a specific strain. The two most well-known cannabinoids are THC (tetrahydrocannabinol) and CBD (cannabidiol). THC is the one that gives cannabis users the psychoactive "high," but CBD has medicinal properties without the side effects. While people looking for non- psychoactive assistance from a variety of medical problems favor CBD-dominant strains, consumers seeking a more muscular and euphoric experience are more likely to gravitate toward strains with higher THC levels.

Cannabis contains fragrant chemicals called terpenes, which give the plant its distinct flavor and aroma. The "entourage effect," wherein the combined presence of these molecules increases the overall medicinal or recreational experience, is known to result from the interaction between terpenes and cannabinoids. Terpene characteristics differ throughout strains; they can be earthy, piney, citrusy, and fruity. Both growers and users value terpene diversity because it adds to the complex effects of individual strains and affects the sensory experience.

The differentiation of cannabis types is further enhanced by the advent of autoflowering strains that are derived from the genetics of Cannabis ruderalis. Based on age, autoflowers automatically switch from vegetative development to flowering, in contrast to standard photoperiod strains that depend on variations in light cycles to start blooming. Because of this feature, growers who want more flexibility in their growing schedules and a quicker turnaround find them especially appealing. Though they can be cultivated indoors and outdoors, auto flowers are often smaller in stature, making them a convenient choice for people with limited time or space.

Breeders and geneticists play a critical role in the ever-growing field of cannabis cultivars. These professionals use selective breeding methods to develop new, enhanced strains with particular traits. The technique entails crossing different parent plants to obtain desirable features, including a higher THC content, distinct tastes, or increased resistance to pests and illnesses. The cannabis market is dynamic due in part to the ongoing innovation in strain production, which offers customers a wide range of options to fit their requirements and preferences.

To sum up, distinguishing between different strains of cannabis requires a thorough comprehension of the architecture, genetic composition, and intricate interactions between terpenes and cannabinoids in the plant. While the classic division of cannabis into indica and sativa offers an essential differentiation, the current cannabis environment acknowledges the need for a more sophisticated approach. An ever-expanding range of cannabis varieties is available for consumers and producers to try, thanks to the rise of hybrid strains, autoflowers, and the focus on cannabinoid and terpene profiles. A thorough grasp of these strains is becoming more and more critical as cannabis production develops, especially for individuals who want to make educated decisions about their cannabis usage and cultivation by navigating the complexity of the cannabis industry.

Choosing the Right Strain for Your Grow

For any cannabis grower, selecting the appropriate strain is essential since it lays the groundwork for an enjoyable and fruitful harvest. With so many different cannabis strains on the market, growers have a wide range of options to choose from, each with a distinct set of effects, flavors, and growth characteristics. Several variables must be carefully considered during this decision-making process, including personal preferences, available space, environmental conditions, and cultivation goals.

The division of cannabis into indica, sativa, and hybrid strains is one of the main differences in strain selection. Because of their calming and soothing qualities, Indica strains are frequently suggested to people who are experiencing stress, anxiety, or sleeplessness. Because Indica plants are often bushier and shorter, they can be grown indoors in environments with limited vertical space. Growers seeking a faster harvest find indica strains appealing because of their typical broad leaves and shorter flowering cycles.

On the other hand, Sativa strains are thought to have stimulating and uplifting properties, making them perfect for daytime use. Sativa plants generally grow taller and more slender, and they do best outside in areas with lots of sunlight. Sativa genetics can be recognized by the extended flowering periods and narrow leaves. Growers seeking a creative and cerebral high frequently gravitate toward sativa strains because they enjoy the mental stimulation and sharpened focus that comes with it.

Indica and sativa traits are crossed to create hybrid strains, which offer a balance between the two strains' finest qualities. Breeders can customize strains to desired characteristics through hybridization, resulting in plants with various flavors, effects, and growth patterns. For those looking for a cross between indica and indica relief or between cerebral and physical effects, hybrid strains provide growers and users with various possibilities.

When considering cannabinoids—the chemical components that the cannabis plant produces—the selection process becomes more sophisticated and goes beyond the superficial classifications of indica, sativa, and hybrid. The two most well-known cannabinoids, tetrahydrocannabinol (THC) and cannabinoid (CBD), each have unique effects. Higher THC strains are linked to the intoxicating "high" that is frequently associated with cannabis use—recreational users who are looking for relaxation and euphoria frequently like these strains. Contrarily, CBD-dominant strains provide medicinal advantages without the high, making them appropriate for people looking to treat a variety of medical ailments without getting high.

Comprehending a strain's cannabinoid profile enables growers to match their cultivation objectives with the desired effects of the finished product. Careful consideration of cannabinoid content is essential when selecting strains, whether the goal is to develop high-THC strains for recreational use or CBD-rich variants for medical use.

Terpenes, which are aromatic molecules present in cannabis, also add a great deal to a strain's overall experience. These substances affect the flavor and aroma of the plant, and when they combine with cannabinoids, they provide the "entourage effect." Terpene characteristics differ throughout strains; they can be earthy, piney, citrusy, and fruity. Strains with particular terpene combinations are prioritized by cultivators who aim to provide a distinctive sensory experience, adding to the variety of flavors and fragrances in the cannabis market.

Environmental circumstances greatly influence strain selection because every strain has different needs and preferences. Because they can be grown inside, indica strains do best in climate-controlled settings with perfectly regulated light, humidity, and temperature cycles. Sativa strains are ideal for outdoor growth since they love bright light and roomier growing environments. Due to their adaptability to indoor and outdoor locations, hybrid strains provide a flexible option for growers with various growth conditions.

Auto-flowering strains, a product of Cannabis ruderalis genetics, further influence the selection of strains. Autoflowers shift the age-dependent from vegetative development to flowering, unlike standard photoperiod strains that depend on variations in light cycles to start flowering. Because of this feature, growers who want more flexibility in their growing schedules and a quicker turnaround find them especially appealing. Autoflowers are a convenient choice for people with limited room or time because they can be cultivated indoors and outdoors despite their generally modest stature.

The intended purpose of the finished product plays a role in selecting a specific strain. To provide solid and euphoric effects, some growers may favor strains with a high THC content for recreational usage. Others might concentrate on CBD-rich strains for medical use, aiming to provide particular therapeutic advantages without inducing a high. The advent of strains designed for specific purposes, including creativity, relaxation, or concentration, also enables growers to match their selections to the intended user experience.

Breeders and geneticists greatly influence the variety and accessibility of cannabis strains. These professionals use selective breeding to improve desired characteristics, such as higher levels of cannabis content, distinctive flavors, or resistance to illnesses and pests. The dynamic nature of the cannabis market is facilitated by the ongoing innovation in strain production, which provides growers and consumers with an ever-expanding range of options to consider.

In summary, selecting the ideal strain for cannabis growing is a complex choice that necessitates a thorough evaluation of several variables. Each component adds to the overall qualities of a strain, from the general classification of indica, sativa, and hybrid strains to the specifics of cannabinoid and terpene profiles. The selection process is further refined by considerations such as intended usage, growing goals, and environmental circumstances, which enable cultivators to make decisions customized to their needs and preferences. Cultivators operate in a dynamic environment where education, experimentation, and a thorough awareness of strain characteristics are vital for fruitful and satisfying cultivation operations, particularly as the cannabis industry continues to expand and diversify.

CHAPTER II

Setting Up Your Grow Space

Indoor vs. Outdoor Cultivation

For cannabis farmers, choosing between indoor and outdoor production is crucial since it affects both the growing environment and the circumstances in which their plants will thrive. Each strategy has its benefits and drawbacks, and the choice ultimately depends on the objectives of the cultivator, the resources at hand, and the surrounding conditions.

Growing indoors provides producers a controlled environment to adjust important parameters like humidity, temperature, and light. This degree of control makes it possible to cultivate year-round, regardless of the outside weather. Artificial lighting systems, including high-pressure sodium (HPS) or light-emitting diode (LED) lights, are frequently used by indoor growers to create the spectrum required for plant growth in both the vegetative and blooming stages. Cultivators can adjust growth rates and environmental conditions to the unique requirements of their selected cannabis strain thanks to this control over light cycles.

Moreover, indoor gardening offers a degree of seclusion and security that is difficult to achieve outside environments. Growers can reduce the risk of theft, vandalism, and unwelcome attention by limiting the cultivation process to an enclosed area. This becomes especially important in areas where there may still be legal prohibitions on the cultivation of cannabis.

On the other hand, indoor gardening has its expenses and difficulties. Setis Expensiventaining an indoor grow room might be costly since you'll need to buy equipment for climate control, lighting, ventilation, and air filtering. The continuous running costs also add a lot to the total cost.

These include power for lighting and environmental control. The requirement for a specific area with enough ventilation and insulation further limits the viability of indoor cultivation for certain people.

On the other hand, outdoor cultivation uses enormous open space and the force of natural sunlight. Sunlight is a plentiful and free resource that gives plants the complete spectrum of light required for healthy growth. Plants grown outside can take advantage of the sun's natural cycle, which fosters strong and healthy growth. In addition, yields per plant are higher in the spacious outside environment than in the cramped indoor grow chamber.

For individuals on a tight budget or cultivating on a larger scale, outdoor cultivation is desirable due to the lower initial setup expenses. Even though security problems are still present in some places, the public nature of outdoor gardening may deter unwelcome attention, particularly when plants are placed in conspicuous places hidden from view. Furthermore, outdoor production uses natural resources instead of energy and does not require inside settings, so its environmental effect is typically more minor.

But cultivating outside is not without its difficulties. Growers are susceptible to temperature swings, unexpected storms, and other climatic factors since they are at the mercy of weather patterns. In an outdoor environment, pests and illnesses can also present serious risks, necessitating close observation and preventative actions to safeguard the crop. Furthermore, the number of harvests per year may be restricted because of the dependence on natural light cycles, particularly in areas with distinct seasons and fewer days.

Further complicating the decision between indoor and outdoor production are the grower's objectives. Those who want exact control over the growing environment and a reliable supply of high-quality, potent cannabis are frequently drawn to indoor farming. Commercial producers seeking a consistent and dependable supply are drawn to the capacity to cultivate year-round and harvest numerous times in a single year.

On the other hand, outdoor growing corresponds with a more conventional and ecologically sensitive strategy. It serves growers who value how their plants work in harmony with the environment to produce distinctive flavors and scents specific to the growing region. Those that grow for personal use frequently choose to cultivate outdoors since it emphasizes a connection to nature and a less intensive, more sustainable method of growing cannabis.

Greenhouse farming, which combines aspects of both indoor and outdoor methods, has become a popular compromise in recent years. In greenhouses, natural sunlight is used to create a regulated atmosphere comparable to indoor horticulture, negating the need for artificial lighting throughout the day. They let some degree of environmental influence on the plants while protecting them from the weather. Additionally, year-round growing in regions with warmer winters is possible with greenhouses.

Ultimately, choosing between indoor and outdoor cultivation is a personal choice that numerous variables impact. Budgetary restrictions, legal issues, the impact on the environment, and the objectives of the cultivation process heavily influence this decision. Some cultivators might even combine the two approaches, using each benefit to develop a flexible and dynamic cultivation plan.

Growers are faced with an increasing number of options as the cannabis industry develops more and as legal frameworks change. Technological developments aid the continuous improvement of these techniques in indoor culture systems and environmentally friendly outdoor production techniques. Selecting between indoor and outdoor cannabis growing is not only a pragmatic option; it also expresses the grower's beliefs, tastes, and goals for their endeavor. Cultivators add to the various tapestry of cannabis cultivation practices, whether in the open air or under the controlled environment of indoor grow lights. Each approach plays a role in defining the business and satisfying the demands of a more discriminating and rising market.

Designing an Efficient Indoor Grow Room

An effective indoor grow room design is essential to growing cannabis because it allows growers to maximize quality and yield while creating the ideal environment for plant growth. Cultivators have unmatched control over critical environmental factors, including light, temperature, humidity, and ventilation, when working indoors. This degree of control makes it possible to cultivate cannabis year-round, regardless of the outside weather, and it offers the chance to customize the growing environment to the unique requirements of the selected strains.

The lighting system is an essential part of the design of an indoor grow room and significantly impacts the growth and development of plants. Due to their effectiveness and affordability, high-intensity discharge (HID) lights, such as metal halide (MH) and high-pressure sodium (HPS) bulbs, have long been used for indoor gardening. HPS lights are mainly well-known for encouraging vigorous flowering, which makes them appropriate for the flowering stage of cannabis development. However, indoor cultivation is changing due to the growing acceptance of light-emitting diode (LED) technology. LED lights have the advantage of being more energy-efficient, having a longer lifespan, and having the light spectrum adjustable to meet the unique requirements of various growth stages. Furthermore, the grow room doesn't require complex cooling systems because LEDs produce less heat.

Controlling humidity and temperature is essential to an indoor grow room's design. Specific temperature and humidity levels are ideal for the growth of cannabis plants, and it is crucial to keep these parameters met. Humidifiers or dehumidifiers control humidity levels while cooling systems like air conditioning or exhaust fans maintain temperature. Finding the ideal balance is significant during the flowering period since imbalances can affect the development of buds and the total output. Plants are given the best circumstances possible throughout their lives thanks to sophisticated temperature control systems that include automated monitoring and adjustments. These systems also help maintain the interior environment's stability and uniformity.

Air circulation is another critical factor in constructing a productive indoor grow room. Enough airflow strengthens plant stems, keeps heat pockets from accumulating, and aids in distributing fresh air, supporting healthy growth. The grow room's carefully positioned oscillating fans guarantee consistent air movement, avoiding stagnant air and lowering the possibility of mold or mildew. Exhaust fans also aid in the plants' general health by eliminating warm and stale air. An environment with adequate ventilation should be prioritized in the design to foster the best possible conditions for transpiration and photosynthesis.

The practical and accurate supply of vital nutrients to the plants is made possible by including nutrient delivery and irrigation systems in the indoor grow room design. Because they improve nutrient uptake and speed up development, hydroponic and aeroponic systems—in which plants thrive in nutrient-rich water without soil—are becoming increasingly popular. These systems frequently have automatic pumps and timers, guaranteeing a steady and dependable flow of nutrients. Even though it is more conventional, soil-based farming necessitates careful consideration of watering techniques and selecting high-quality, well-draining soil. Irrigation solutions that complement the chosen growing technique should be incorporated into the design to assist optimal root development and nutrient absorption.

Optimizing the layout and utilizing available space are essential components of a successful indoor grow room design. Plants, lighting, and equipment should be arranged to maximize as much space as possible while being easily accessible and maintained. Techniques for vertical cultivation, like trellising systems or vertical racks, make the most of the limited floor area while distributing light evenly throughout the lower canopy levels. Effective utilization of available space also encompasses the arrangement of apparatus, guaranteeing that every part is positioned to reduce disruption to plant development and enable effortless observation and modification.

An important factor in improving the effectiveness of indoor grow room design is reflective surfaces. Light is reflected onto the plants by walls and ceilings coated in reflective materials like Mylar or white paint, which stops the light from being absorbed by nearby objects. By doing this, you can ensure that the plant canopy receives the most light possible, maximizing light efficiency and encouraging uniform development. Reflective surfaces help the lighting system function more efficiently overall by enabling growers to attain the best possible fair coverage and intensity across the grow room.

The way indoor grow rooms are planned and run is changing due to automation and technological integration. The margin of error in cultivation procedures is decreased by the precision and consistency provided by automated systems for lighting, climate management, and fertilizer supply. Growers may remotely examine and modify environmental conditions with the help of timers, sensors, and monitoring devices, giving them real-time insights into the health of their plants. Innovative technology increases overall efficiency by streamlining the growing process and allowing growers to maximize resource use, reduce manual intervention, and maximize overall growth.

When designing indoor grow rooms, security is of utmost importance, particularly in areas where cannabis growth is associated with legal restrictions or societal stigmas. Robust security measures are implemented to safeguard the integrity of the cultivation operation and the cultivator's investment. Secure entry points, access controls, and surveillance systems help create a safe environment by preventing unwanted entry and protecting the grow room's priceless possessions. Furthermore, the secure storage of gardening supplies and equipment guarantees the preservation of invaluable resources.

An adequate indoor grow room should be designed to consider the changing legal environment around cannabis growth. Ensuring the viability and legitimacy of the cultivation operation requires adherence to local rules, such as zoning laws, electricity codes, and licensing requirements. These legal factors should be considered during the design process to create a framework that complies with regulations and makes it easy to follow the law.

In conclusion, creating a productive indoor grow space is a complex process that requires a thorough evaluation of several variables. Every component, from space usage and security measures to lighting systems and environmental controls, is vital to the overall performance of the growing operation. Cultivators now have unprecedented opportunities to develop complex, automated, and environmentally controlled settings that optimize plant growth and maximum production, thanks to the ongoing advancements in technology and cultivating practices. The design of indoor grow rooms represents both the pursuit of horticultural excellence and the agility and innovation needed to succeed in a dynamic and competitive cultivation environment as the cannabis business evolves and legal environments change.

Creating an Ideal Outdoor Growing Environment

For cannabis growers, designing the perfect outdoor growing space is a complex and satisfying process that can lead to vigorous, sun-loving plants and a connection to the natural world. In contrast to indoor gardening, outdoor growing uses sunlight and a roomy outdoor environment to promote the growth of healthy plants. The best outdoor environment design considers the weather, soil, sunshine exposure, water availability, and safety precautions.

The climate is one of the main elements affecting the performance of outdoor cultivation. Specific temperature ranges are ideal for cannabis plants, and the local climate strongly influences their development. Growers need to be aware of the environment in the area, including variations in temperature, precipitation patterns, and the growing season's duration. It is crucial to choose cannabis strains compatible with the local climate to maximize productivity and ensure the plants can tolerate environmental stresses.

When designing the perfect outdoor growing habitat, sunlight exposure is an essential factor to consider. Because cannabis plants are photoperiodic, their transition from the vegetative to flowering stages is triggered by variations in the length of daylight. Selecting a spot that receives lots of sunlight is essential for producing robust, healthy plants. Slopes facing south or places with little shade are ideal for getting the most sunshine exposure possible all day. Furthermore, growers must consider the sun's path across the sky at various times of the year, strategically positioning plants to use the available sunlight.

An essential component of outdoor cultivation's success is soil quality. Cannabis plants need soil that drains properly and has a balanced nutrient content. Tests are conducted to determine the soil's pH levels and nutrient content to help growers make educated decisions about fertilization and soil amendments. Compost and other organic matter can improve the structure and nutrient retention of the soil, creating a rich environment for plant development. Raised beds and container gardening are additional options for cultivators, giving them more control over drainage and soil quality.

Having access to water is essential for creating the perfect outdoor growing space. Cannabis plants require a sufficient amount of water, particularly in times of extreme heat or drought. Outdoor agriculture requires both an effective irrigation system and access to a consistent water supply. Plants can be consistently and carefully watered with drip irrigation or soaker hoses, which minimizes the chance of overwatering or underwatering. By keeping soil moisture around plants, mulching reduces evaporative water loss.

The local environment and the cultivator's desired effects play a role in selecting cannabis strains for outdoor cultivation. In areas with shorter growing seasons or colder climates, Indica strains are frequently preferred due to their sturdy structures and shorter flowering times. Sativa strains do well in warmer climates with longer growing seasons because of their longer flowering times and taller growth. Indica and sativa qualities are combined in hybrid strains to provide a medium ground. Growers can use the natural elements to attain the best outcomes by choosing strains specifically suited to the outside environment.

Security precautions are essential when designing the perfect outdoor growing space, especially in areas where cannabis growth is associated with legal restrictions or societal stigmas. They safeguard confidentiality and prevent unwanted entry to prevent plant theft and damage. The cultivation location can be hidden from curious eyes by strategically planting natural barriers or planting companion crops. Security cameras, fencing, and access restrictions can be implemented to enhance the security of the outside environment further and protect the investment and integrity of the growing operation.

Companion planting and crop rotation are two sustainable techniques that improve the resilience and well-being of the outdoor growing environment. Crops of cannabis that are rotated with other plants help keep pests and illnesses that are unique to cannabis from growing. Plants that complement or repel one another are intentionally placed to increase biodiversity and create a more balanced ecosystem through companion planting. For instance, growing fragrant flowers or herbs close to cannabis plants may help keep pests away and create a healthier outdoor space.

Because it coincides with the natural growing season and the lifecycle of cannabis plants, timing is an essential component of outdoor cultivation. Timing the planting and harvesting of your plants requires understanding the length of the growing season and the dates of the local frost. Before moving seeds outside, cultivators can use the best growth window by starting seeds indoors or germinating in a greenhouse. This guarantees that plants are well-established before encountering the outdoor environment's difficulties.

Growers may look into the usage of greenhouses or hoop houses to extend the growth season in areas where the length of the outdoor growing season is restricted by weather. These structures let plants get natural sunlight while offering a certain degree of climate control. In addition to the benefits of outdoor growing, greenhouses provide environmental control by shielding plants from inclement weather like heavy rain or high winds.

Creating the perfect outdoor growing environment requires community involvement and ethical cultivation techniques. Growers need to be aware of the potential effects that their operations may have on the environment and communities around them. Strong relationships throughout the neighborhood are fostered by maintaining open contact with neighbors, adhering to local regulations, and eliminating potential nuisances like odor.

Sustainable growth techniques, such as organic growing and water conservation, further demonstrate a commitment to ethical and environmentally friendly cannabis farming.

In conclusion, designing the perfect outdoor growing space requires careful consideration of combining sustainable methods, natural components, and a thorough grasp of the ecosystem and climate of the area. Cultivators must negotiate several concerns to promote vibrant and healthy cannabis plants, from choosing the correct strains to optimizing sunshine exposure, soil quality, and water management. Timing concerns, security protocols, and community involvement complete the diverse approach to outdoor farming. The ideal outdoor growing environment is designed to show a dedication to horticultural excellence and a harmonic integration with the surrounding community and environment as the cannabis business matures.

CHAPTER III

Essential Grow Equipment

Lighting Systems

Effective lighting systems are essential to good cultivation techniques because they supply the energy required for photosynthesis and significantly impact the general growth and development of plants. Choosing the right lighting system is especially important when growing cannabis since exact control over the growing environment is essential. Cultivators have various lighting options, including the increasingly common light-emitting diode (LED) technology and more conventional high-intensity discharge (HID) lights. The advantages, disadvantages, and considerations that come with each lighting system influence the growth process for both hobbyists and commercial growers.

Because of their effectiveness and affordability, high-intensity discharge (HID) lights have long been a mainstay in indoor cannabis growing. High-pressure sodium (HPS) and metal halide (MH) lights are the two primary types of HID lights frequently utilized during various stages of plant growth. HPS lights are well-liked for the blooming phase of cannabis cultivation because they emit a spectrum of light that is especially favorable to flowering and fruiting. In contrast, metal halide lamps provide a spectrum that is more in line with blue wavelengths, making them appropriate for the vegetative growth stage when plants concentrate on developing leaves.

Even though HID lights have shown to be dependable workhorses for indoor gardening, they have certain shortcomings. A notable disadvantage is their comparatively elevated heat output. Complex cooling systems must be installed to keep the grow room at the ideal temperature due to the high heat produced by HID lights. The extra heat adds to the overall operating costs of indoor cultivation and increases energy consumption. In addition, HID lights need more maintenance and replacements more frequently than LEDs or other more modern technologies because of their shorter lifespan.

Light-emitting diode (LED) technology has been more well-known in cannabis farming in recent years, completely changing the indoor growing environment. Several benefits that LED lights provide offset some of the drawbacks of HID lighting. The energy efficiency of LEDs is one of their main advantages. LEDs use less heat and more efficiency to generate light, so they use less electricity and don't require as many sophisticated cooling systems. In addition to reducing operating expenses, this enhanced energy efficiency aligns with the growing emphasis on environmentally friendly and sustainable farming methods.

LED lights are renowned for having much longer lifespans than conventional HID lights. Over time, the reduced frequency of replacements due to this durability results in cost savings. Furthermore, growers can tailor the light spectrum to meet the requirements of various growth phases by designing LED lights to emit particular wavelengths of light. Cultivators can maximize the light conditions for both the vegetative and flowering phases thanks to this spectrum management, which may enhance their plants' general health and productivity.

Although LED fixtures often have a more significant starting cost than HID lights, they usually pay for themselves in energy savings, lower maintenance requirements, and better spectrum control over time. Full-spectrum LEDs and customizable spectrum controls are two examples of advances becoming more common in the LED technology environment. By attempting to capture the complete spectrum of sunshine, full-spectrum LEDs offer a more all-encompassing light source that more nearly resembles the environmental circumstances in which cannabis plants need to flourish.

The length of light exposure, or photoperiod, significantly impacts the growth and blooming patterns of cannabis plants, in addition to the choice between HID and LED lights. Since cannabis is a photoperiodic plant, variations in the length of daylight cause it to go from a vegetative to a blooming state. It is standard practice to use a longer light cycle of 18 to 24 hours each day during the vegetative stage when plants concentrate on leafy growth. Cultivators instruct the plants to focus their energy on developing flowers by reducing the light cycle to 12 hours of light and 12 hours of darkness as they begin the flowering stage.

One of the most important aspects of growing cannabis is adjusting photoperiod, which is especially important for indoor producers who have control over the length and intensity of light exposure. In contrast, the photoperiod is naturally determined by the changing seasons and natural sunshine for outdoor cultivators. The ability of auto-flowering strains, a relatively new breed of cannabis, to go into flowering depending only on age rather than variations in light cycles has made them famous. Because of this trait, autoflowers grow well outside and offer more options to interior producers who want faster turnaround times.

Light movers and reflectors are crucial add-ons for indoor gardening since they increase the coverage and effectiveness of lighting systems. To help direct and focus light onto the plant canopy and stop it from being absorbed by surrounding surfaces, reflectors are frequently placed above the lights. By ensuring that a more significant proportion of the light emitted reaches the plants, this reflecting efficiency maximizes photosynthesis and total development. To further improve light distribution and minimize uneven coverage, light movers actively move the light source around the grow space, ensuring that every section of the canopy receives enough sunlight.

The distance between the light source and the plant canopy, in addition to the kind of light and its duration, is a critical factor in deciding how effective the lighting system is. The inverse square law governs the relationship between light intensity and distance, which states that light intensity decreases with the square of the distance from the source. This indicates that the amount of light that reaches the plants rapidly decreases with increasing distance from the light source. It is crucial to keep the lights and canopy at the ideal distance to avoid light burn or inadequate light penetration, both of which can have detrimental effects on the health and productivity of the plants.

The management and monitoring of lighting systems in indoor cultivation is changing due to the integration of automation and intelligent technology. Cultivators can carefully control the photoperiod by using automated systems with programmable timers and light controllers to alter the length and intensity of light exposure according to the needs of individual plants. These systems also allow for remote monitoring, giving growers access to real-time data on lighting conditions so they may make any necessary adjustments immediately. Smart technology integration helps with resource optimization, energy efficiency, and streamlining farming procedures.

The selection and operation of lighting systems are increasingly influenced by environmental sustainability. Growers are looking for methods to adopt eco-friendly practices and lessen their environmental impact as the cannabis business grows. Since LED technology offers energy-efficient solutions that reduce power usage and greenhouse gas emissions, it is a good fit for ecological goals. In addition, developments in energy-saving lighting, such as quantum boards and efficient driver technologies, support an indoor cultivation strategy that is more environmentally friendly.

To sum up, lighting systems are essential to the success of cannabis farming since they affect the plant during its whole life cycle, from germination to harvest. Deciding between current light-emitting diode (LED) technology and conventional high-intensity discharge (HID) lighting is crucial for farmers. Each option has pros and downsides of its own. The adjustment of the photoperiod further enhances the complex art and science of cannabis production, the separation of the light source and canopy, and the use of intelligent technology. Lighting systems are essential for guiding innovation in sustainable and effective cannabis production, guaranteeing optimal plant health, and influencing cultivating techniques as the cannabis business develops.

Ventilation and Air Circulation

Whether growing cannabis indoors or outdoors, proper ventilation and air movement are necessary for a productive setup. The flow of air through the produce area is essential for controlling the temperature, humidity, and carbon dioxide (CO2) content, all of which significantly impact the well-being, development, and general output of cannabis plants.

Maintaining an atmosphere that is favorable for cultivation indoors requires enough ventilation. The procedure removes heat, humidity, and stale air from the growing area and replaces it with fresh air. Stagnant air can produce pockets of high humidity, which can hinder plant transpiration and nutrient absorption and cause problems with mold and mildew. Regulating air exchange promotes a more stable and healthy atmosphere by reducing these difficulties.

To provide a constant airflow, ventilation systems typically include ductwork, intake and exhaust vents, and fans. Exhaust fans remove Warm, humid air from the growing area, keeping it from building up and negatively impacting the plants. By allowing fresh air to enter the room, intake vents help to maintain the ideal equilibrium. Air must circulate evenly throughout the grow room thanks to the assistance of ductwork in directing air movement. Furthermore, odors can be eliminated from ventilation systems by integrating carbon filters, an essential factor to consider in areas where cannabis cultivation is subject to legal limitations or privacy concerns.

Sufficient ventilation is essential when cannabis plants are in blossom since they release powerful, unique scents at that time. Effective odor control adds to the cultivation area's overall comfort while encouraging discretion. Cultivators may properly manage ventilation and create an atmosphere where cannabis plants thrive without unnecessary stress by balancing intake and exhaust and adding carbon filters.

Ventilation is essential for controlling temperature and humidity and maximizing carbon dioxide (CO2) availability, a necessary component of photosynthesis. Through photosynthesis, plants transform CO2 into carbohydrates, oxygen, light, and water. To accelerate the growth of cannabis plants in an indoor environment, where CO2 concentrations can gradually decrease, more CO2 can be added. Adequate ventilation guarantees that CO2 is distributed uniformly, which keeps plants from stagnating and gives them access to the vital gas required for vigorous photosynthesis.

Air circulation concentrates on air movement around the plants, whereas ventilation mainly deals with air exchange within an interior environment. More vigorous plant stems, the avoidance of heat pockets, and the uniform distribution of CO2 and fresh air all depend on proper air circulation. A grow room's well-placed oscillating fans encourage consistent air movement, eliminating stagnant air and fostering a climate that allows cannabis plants to transpire effectively.

Plants absorb nutrients and regulate their temperature through the process of transpiration, which involves the release of water vapor through their leaves. Effective transpiration is made possible by efficient air circulation, guaranteeing that plants can absorb nutrients and water efficiently. Stagnant air can hinder transpiration, resulting in problems including vitamin shortages, heat stress, and a greater vulnerability to illnesses and pests. Oscillating fans create a soft airflow that replicates the wind that naturally occurs outside, fortifying plant structures and fostering ideal growth conditions.

Geographical factors and wind patterns are two natural components that affect air circulation in outdoor agriculture. Cultivators can carefully arrange plants to maximize exposure to prevailing breezes, even though they have less direct control over outdoor air circulation than indoors. Air circulates naturally in a balanced outdoor environment, enhanced by planting in open spaces and using windbreaks to protect against severe winds.

Proper ventilation and air circulation are especially crucial because there is a higher risk of mold and mildew in areas with high humidity. Successful outdoor growing involves choosing strains resistant to moisture-related problems, pruning to increase air movement beneath the canopy, and leaving enough space between plants. Cultivators can also use strategies like trellising to support plant structures and improve air circulation, which lowers the possibility of humidity-related issues.

With greenhouses, growers may use natural sunshine while keeping an environment under control, providing a medium ground between indoor and outdoor cultivation. In greenhouse agriculture, adequate ventilation and air circulation are essential for combining the advantages of external exposure with the control of indoor conditions. Exhaust fans, ridge vents, and side vents with louvers all aid in controlling temperature and humidity. In contrast, horizontal airflow fans ensure that the greenhouse air is evenly distributed. Cannabis plants can thrive in an environment with controlled air conditions and sunshine combined with natural and mechanical ventilation.

Cultivators should also consider the effect of air movement and ventilation on plant transpiration rates. Excessively fast transpiration can cause dehydration and water stress, while high transpiration rates can aid in cooling and nutrient absorption. Cultivators can create an environment where transpiration happens ideally without unnecessarily burdening the plants by monitoring and changing ventilation systems.

Cultivators can adjust ventilation and air circulation using automated controls and sensor-equipped environmental control systems. These systems enable real-time modifications to maintain the optimum conditions by monitoring temperature, humidity, CO2 levels, and even air movement. The precision of cultivation procedures is improved by automated controls, which allow growers to tailor the growing environment to the unique requirements of their cannabis plants.

In summary, proper ventilation and air circulation are essential for growing cannabis since they affect plant health, growth rates, and overall yield. A steady and favorable atmosphere for cannabis plants can be created by carefully controlling air exchange and movement in indoor, outdoor, or greenhouse settings. Appropriate ventilation and air circulation are essential for fostering a climate that allows cannabis plants to flourish, as they minimize mold and mildew and enhance effective transpiration and nutrient absorption. Cultivators use sustainable techniques and technological breakthroughs to improve and optimize ventilation systems as the cannabis industry develops, which adds to the overall sustainability and success of cannabis production methods.

Nutrients and Soil Amendments

An essential component of cannabis growing, nutrients and soil amendments significantly impact plant health, growth, and, eventually, the quality of the finished product. Like other plants, cannabis needs a wide range of nutrients to flourish, and cultivating in the soil means adjusting the soil composition to provide the ideal environment for nutrient uptake. This section examines the vital role that nutrients and soil amendments play in the growth of cannabis, examining the fundamental components, their purposes, and the significance of creating a growing medium that is both balanced and nutrient-rich.

The key to growing cannabis well is knowing which bare macronutrients plants need in relatively significant amounts. These macronutrients, potassium (K), phosphorus (P), and nitrogen (N), are the building blocks of the NPK ratio that is frequently seen on fertilizer labels. Nitrogen is essential for vegetative growth because it encourages thick stems and luxuriant foliage. Phosphorus is crucial during the flowering stage since it is necessary for root growth and blossom development. Potassium contributes to the production of carbohydrates and helps plants withstand stress, which promotes overall plant health.

Cannabis plants also need supplementary nutrients, though in smaller quantities than macronutrients. Sulfur, calcium, and magnesium are regarded as secondary nutrients, and they all have distinct functions in the growth of plants. Calcium is necessary to synthesize cell walls and general structural integrity. A key component of chlorophyll, magnesium aids in photosynthesis and the movement of energy throughout the plant. Sulfur is involved in synthesizing vitamins and enzymes and is essential for creating amino acids.

Even though they are only slightly necessary, micronutrients are just as crucial for cannabis plants. Micronutrients such as iron, manganese, zinc, copper, boron, and molybdenum are involved in several physiological processes. These micronutrients affect nutrient transport within the plant, act as enzyme cofactors, and participate in redox processes. A balanced supply of these micronutrients is necessary to avoid deficiencies that can cause growth retardation or chlorosis, two conditions that are visible signs.

Although some nutrients are naturally present in the soil, effective cannabis production frequently necessitates adding fertilizers to the soil to suit the unique requirements of the plants. Fertilizers are available in many formulas, such as organic and synthetic. Because synthetic fertilizers are made to include exact nutrient ratios, growers can customize the nutritional profile to the plants' growth stage. Because they come from natural sources, organic fertilizers have a more varied nutrient profile and support microbial activity and nutrient cycling, improving soil health.

Soil amendments, in addition to fertilizers, are essential for improving the structure and fertility of the growing medium. Organic or inorganic materials can be added to the soil as soil supplements to enhance its physical characteristics, water retention ability, and nutrient-holding capacity. Compost, well-rotted manure, and cover crops are examples of organic amendments that provide organic matter to the soil, boosting microbial activity and improving soil structure. Inorganic additives, such as vermiculite or perlite, enhance aeration and drainage, avoiding compaction and guaranteeing that roots receive oxygen.

Cultivators frequently test their soil to evaluate the nutrient composition of their growing medium and make decisions about the kind and quantity of fertilizers and amendments required. Cultivators can make well-informed adjustments to produce the ideal growing environment by using the valuable insights that soil testing offers regarding the soil's pH, nutrient levels, and overall composition. Maintaining the proper pH level is very important since it affects nutritional availability. Soils with a pH range of 6.0 to 7.0 that are slightly acidic to neutral are generally ideal for cannabis plant growth. Variations from this range may result in toxicities or nutrient shortages, which may impact the health and growth of plants.

Soilless growing techniques, such as hydroponics and coco coir, allow for fine control over nutrient supply and do away with the need for traditional soil. Nutrient solutions are delivered straight to the roots of plants in hydroponic systems, completely obviating the need for soil. Cultivators may achieve unmatched control over pH levels, fertilizer concentrations, and general environmental conditions with this technology. Another well-liked soilless alternative is coco coir, a coconut fiber medium with good aeration, neutral pH, and water retention qualities.

Organic farming methods strongly emphasize nourishing the land and plants with sustainable, natural inputs. Compost, green manure, and cover crops are essential to organic farming because they increase microbial diversity and soil fertility. When the soil is unused, cover crops, like grasses or legumes, are sown to fix nitrogen, enhance soil structure, and stop erosion. By adding new plant material to the soil, green manure helps to increase the amount of organic matter and improves nutrient availability. A mixture of organic debris broken down into compost adds vital nutrients to the soil and fosters a thriving soil ecology.

Growing cannabis holistically entails considering the interactions between nutrients, soil health, and the plant's life cycle. Cannabis plants require more nitrogen during vegetative to maintain their rapid growth. Balanced formulas with a higher nitrogen content are usually preferred during this stage. Phosphorus and potassium become increasingly important when plants enter the flowering stage, affecting bud development and total flower production. An essential method in the production of cannabis is to modify the ratios of nutrients according to the particular requirements of every stage of growth.

Nutrient imbalances and overfertilization can cause nutrient toxicity, lockout, and other undesirable effects in cannabis plants. A careful balance between giving plants enough nutrients and not overdoing it, which can be harmful to the health of the plants, must be struck by cultivators. Farmers can adjust fertilizer regimens by routinely checking plants for nutrient excess or deficiency indicators, such as leaf discoloration, stunted growth, or irregular flowering.

Cannabis plants also display varying dietary needs according to their genetic composition or strain. Known for their tall height and extended blooming durations, Sativa-dominant strains may have different nutrient requirements than Indica-dominant strains, which are smaller in stature and blossom more quickly. Due to their genetic makeup, hybrid strains, which mix sativa and indica qualities, offer a range of nutrient requirements.

Cultivators often add natural soil additives to improve fertility when cultivating outdoors, where plants interact with the local soil. In addition to fixing nitrogen, cover crops like legumes and clover help shield the soil from erosion and serve as a home for beneficial insects. Adding organic matter gradually, controlling temperature, and preserving soil moisture are all aided by mulching with organic materials like wood chips or straw. These environmentally friendly methods support the soil's long-term stability and outdoor farming's general sustainability.

To sum up, nutrients and soil amendments are essential to a good cannabis crop since they influence the health, development, and quality of the finished product of the plants. Properly controlling nutrient profiles and soil conditions is crucial whether growing in soil, soilless media, or using organic methods.

Cannabis plants are given the nutrients they need for optimum growth when macronutrients, secondary nutrients, and micronutrients are balanced and the soil's pH and general composition are considered. Cultivators use developments in soil amendments, fertilizer formulations, and sustainable practices to improve their cultivation techniques and add to the overall sustainability and success of cannabis production as the cannabis industry continues to change.

CHAPTER IV

Germination and Propagation

Germination Techniques

A crucial phase of the life cycle of cannabis plants is germination, which signals the beginning of the transition from seed to solid and vibrant plants. A plentiful harvest and healthy development are predicated on successful germination. Cannabis growers utilize diverse methods to guarantee ideal germination, considering elements like seed caliber, surrounding circumstances, and appropriate germination media. The complexities of germination techniques in cannabis production are examined in this section, along with the significance of proper procedures and essential factors that affect the outcome of this first stage.

A key element affecting the success of germination is seed quality. Premium cannabis seeds, such as a mature, well-defined shape, a firm, undamaged shell, and a dark color, share certain traits. Growers prioritize these characteristics when choosing seeds for germination since they show viability and vigor. Fresher seeds often have higher germination rates; thus, the seeds' age also matters. Purchasing seeds from trustworthy vendors guarantees that growers will have the best genetic material available when germination begins.

Providing the ideal climatic conditions for cannabis seeds to initiate the emergence of a new plant is one of the basic germination strategies. Seeds can be germinated in a damp, sterile media or between moist paper towels, which cultivators frequently use. By establishing a regulated environment, this method promotes water absorption and starts the metabolic processes of the seed. To mimic soil properties, the seeds are layered between wet paper towel layers and left in the dark. It is essential to keep the environment continually moist to assist the early stages of germination.

Sowing cannabis seeds directly into a growth medium is another well-liked approach for getting them to germinate. Seeds can be planted now in soil that has been pre-moistened or in soilless media like peat pellets or coco coir. By simulating how seeds naturally germinate in the soil, this method enables a smooth transition as the seedling appears and takes root. A fungal disease called damping off, which can harm young seedlings, can be prevented by keeping the growing media continuously moist but not soggy.

Humidity and temperature are critical for adequate germination. For cannabis seeds to begin germination, a warm, humid atmosphere is typically needed. For most cannabis strains, a temperature range of 70–85°F (21–29°C) is thought to be ideal. To keep a consistently favorable temperature for germination, cultivators frequently employ techniques like setting seed trays on heat mats. Keeping the humidity high—between 70 and 90 percent—also contributes to developing an environment encouraging water absorption and seedling emergence.

Another essential factor to consider during germination is light conditions. Cannabis seeds are not light-sensitive during the first stages of germination, but they are as soon as the seedlings appear. A steady, mild light source—such as fluorescent or LED lights—helps keep seedlings from growing too long and promotes strong development. As seedlings age and are ready for the vegetative stage, cultivators frequently move them to brighter lighting.

A taproot and cotyledon leaves appear during germination, which usually lasts a few days. The seedling is prepared for transplanting into a larger container or the preferred growing medium once it has grown to a suitable size and appears robust and healthy. Because of their fragility, seedlings must be handled carefully when transplanted to prevent harm to the developing root system and early shoots.

Some gardeners experiment with cutting-edge approaches, including pre-soaking seeds in a solution of water and hydrogen peroxide in addition to conventional germination methods. This technique aims to improve water absorption and offer a barrier of defense against any infections. Before the seeds are placed in the germination medium, they are soaked for a certain amount—typically no longer than 24 hours. Although some growers have found success with this method, it needs to be done precisely and under close supervision to avoid over-soaking, which can negatively impact the viability of the seeds.

In addition, growers of cannabis experiment with different methods of germination, like scarification. Scarification is lightly abrading the seed's exterior shell by nicking it or delicately sanding it. This process speeds up water absorption and promotes taproot development. Although scarification has advantages in some situations, it must be done carefully to prevent undue damage to the seed.

Another technique that growers use is seed stratification, especially for some cannabis strains that could benefit from a cold treatment phase. This method entails exposing seeds to low temperatures for a predetermined time, usually in a refrigerator. For some seed strains that naturally thrive in more relaxed environments, stratification is hypothesized to disrupt seed dormancy and increase germination rates. However, not all cannabis seeds need to be stratified, so before using this technique, ensure you understand the particular needs of the strain you've selected.

One crucial factor that can significantly impact how well the germination process goes is the selection of the germination medium. Since traditional soil has essential minerals and is naturally composed, it is still a favored medium for cannabis seed germination. Cultivators frequently use a light, airy potting mix that encourages proper drainage and aeration. Soilless mediums, including peat pellets or coco coir, offer substitutes that have comparable advantages and permit more

Exact control over the retention of water. Hydroponics

and aeroponics provide a nutrient-rich solution to developing plants, eliminating the need for soil during germination. The water-based medium used in these systems enables fine control over pH and nutrient contents. Hydroponic and aeroponic techniques, however less prevalent for germination, can be advantageous in that they can provide early fertilizer delivery and adequate water and nutrient uptake.

For the seedling to successfully emerge from the germination phase, adequate hydration must be maintained. Issues impacting seed viability and developing seedlings' health can arise from overwatering or underwatering. Maintaining a steady, reasonable degree of hydration and keeping a close eye on the moisture content of the germination medium is crucial. The amount of water needed at this stage depends on several variables, including temperature, humidity in the surrounding air, and the particulars of the selected germination strategy.

Cloning Strategies

Cloning is a standard method used in cannabis farming that enables cultivators to create genetically identical plants from a mother plant while maintaining the desired characteristics of a particular strain. Many benefits come with this technique, such as maintaining constant genetics, yielding consistent crops, and effectively propagating plants with specified traits. Cloning is a valuable technique for hobbyists and commercial growers who want to maximize yield and simplify their operations. This section examines the several cloning techniques used in cannabis cultivation, looking at the supplies, equipment, and techniques used by growers to multiply plants by cloning successfully.

Using cuttings from a healthy, mature cannabis plant is one of the simplest and most popular methods for cloning. These cuttings, frequently called clones or clones, are picked with care from a mother plant's lower branches. The chosen branches should be in the vegetative stage, thriving, and showing no symptoms of disease, stress, or pests. Growers frequently select branches with well- developed nodes since they are the areas from which roots will originate, which increases the likelihood of success throughout the cloning process.

Growers use various techniques to promote root formation on these clones when cuttings are chosen. A popular method is immersing the clone's cut end into a solution called rooting hormone, which includes auxins to promote the formation of roots. Rooting hormones aid in hastening the emergence of roots on cuttings and come in gel, liquid, or powder form. The clones are planted in a suitable growing medium—soil or a soilless mix—after the rooting hormone has been applied to supply vital nutrients and encourage the growth of roots.

Using aeroponic or hydroponic systems made especially for rooting cuttings is another well-liked cloning technique. These devices encourage quick root formation by suspending clones in a nutrient-rich mist or nutrient solution. The advantages of both hydroponic and aeroponic cloning systems include precise control over fertilizer delivery, enhanced oxygen availability, and quicker root initiation. These systems are prevalent in commercial contexts where uniformity and efficiency are essential for large-scale cloning operations.

For cloning to be successful, the proper environmental parameters must be maintained. Elevated humidity levels, commonly attained through a propagation tray or a humidity dome, foster the growth of roots and lessen water loss through transpiration by creating a microenvironment. Maintaining a consistent and comfortable temperature, often 72–78°F (22–26°C), aids in cloning. Sufficient illumination, commonly offered by fluorescent or LED lights featuring a spectrum appropriate for vegetative development, guarantees that the clones obtain the energy required for root formation while reducing strain.

Tissue culture propagation is an advanced cloning process that is becoming increasingly common. Through tissue culture, plant cells or tissues are cultivated in a sterile, controlled environment. To start a cannabis tissue culture, tiny tissue samples are removed from a mother plant and put in an agar media that is high in nutrients. With the help of this technique, several genetically identical plants can be produced in a sterile, disease-free environment. Tissue culture offers benefits in terms of mass production, disease removal, and long-term preservation of rare genetic strains despite requiring specialized equipment and knowledge.

Selecting the appropriate mother plant is essential when cloning a plant. The mother plant provides the clones with genetic material, and the mother plant's traits significantly impact the quality of the plants that come from it. Expert growers choose mother plants by considering characteristics including potency, vigor, yield, and disease and insect resistance. The effectiveness of the cloning process largely depends on the mother plant's health being regularly monitored and any plants exhibiting signs of stress or genetic abnormalities being removed.

On their mother plants, cultivators frequently use a method called topping to promote lateral branching and develop a bushier, more robust structure. When the apical or core shoot is removed, several colas and lateral branches grow due to topping. This procedure produces more branches ideal for cloning and increases the mother plant's overall yield. Cuttings taken from topped plants usually have more developed nodes and are more likely to root successfully.

Regular cloning is routine for cultivators, who keep a specific area for mother plants. This enables producers to provide the mother plants with the best possible environment, guaranteeing their long-term health and productivity. Mother plants are frequently preserved in the vegetative stage by giving them 18 to 24 hours of light daily on a continuous cycle. The mother plants remain a constant source of cuttings because of the prolonged light cycle that keeps them from blossoming.

Cultivators utilize diverse tactics to optimize the

effectiveness and prosperity of their cloning endeavors. Using a cloning gel or solution that contains nutrients and rooting hormones to encourage the growth of roots is one such tactic. Before planting in the growing media, these gels or solutions are directly applied to the clone's cut end. The clones have an early advantage in establishing themselves since the cloning gel contains nutrients that are necessary to assist the formation of their roots.

Clone propagation relies heavily on timing, with growers selecting particular phases of plant growth for best results. Although cuttings can be taken from clones at any growth stage, many growers prefer to take cuttings when the plants are vegetative, actively growing, and showing good health. Cloning is frequently timed by the overall cultivation timetable, guaranteeing the clones enough time to root and reach the vegetative stage before flowering.

Practicing good hygiene throughout the cloning procedure is critical to avoid introducing germs that could endanger the clones' health. Contamination can be reduced by sterilizing instruments like razor blades and scissors before taking cuttings. Wearing gloves and maintaining a sterile and clean atmosphere when working with clones minimizes the possibility of introducing dangerous microbes. Disease control is significant in large-scale commercial operations, where the rapid spread of infections can have serious repercussions.

Additionally, growers experiment with cutting-edge techniques to improve cloning productivity, like using specialized cloning equipment. These devices give the clones a regulated environment with regular illumination, humidity, and misting to encourage root development. Cloning machines are made to automate and simplify the cloning process so growers can produce a lot of clones with little work. Cloning machines are convenient, but they may need to be closely watched to guarantee the right conditions for root formation.

In addition to standard cloning techniques, growers can try other approaches, including air layering or grafting. Air layering entails forcing roots to develop on a branch while it is still linked to the mother plant to separate a rooted clone. By grafting, two distinct plants' tissues are combined to produce a new plant with the desired traits. Although less common in cannabis production, these techniques demonstrate the innovation and adaptability of producers looking for novel propagation methods.

Ensuring Healthy Seedlings

A key component of growing cannabis successfully is starting with healthy seedlings, which create the conditions for solid growth, maximum yields, and a bountiful crop. Going from seed to seedling is an important one that requires close consideration of several variables, such as seed quality, germination methods, environmental circumstances, and post-germination maintenance. This section examines the critical factors and tactics used by cannabis growers to promote the health and vigor of seedlings, acknowledging the vital role that these plants play in the cultivation process' ultimate success.

To ensure the health of your seedlings, start with premium cannabis seeds. Seed quality significantly influences Germination rates and seedlings' subsequent growth. Skilled growers prefer seeds with desired characteristics, such as a mature appearance, a black and undamaged outer shell, and a track record of reliable germination. Purchasing seeds from trustworthy and dependable vendors is crucial since it guarantees genetic stability and the lack of pollutants or congenital abnormalities. High-quality seeds enable farmers to optimize their plants' potential, laying the groundwork for a successful growing journey.

When a seed becomes a seedling, germination processes are essential. Cultivators can start germination in several ways, such as using wet paper towels, directly planting in growing media, or using specialized germination systems. Variables like cultivation scale, personal desire, and resource availability frequently influence the selection of germination technique. Maintaining ideal circumstances is crucial, regardless of the strategy used. Several variables, including light, humidity, temperature, and rooting hormone application, are necessary for good germination and the development of robust seedlings.

The health and vigor of the plants are greatly influenced by the environmental factors present throughout the germination and early seedling phases. Keeping the atmosphere warm and humid replicates the circumstances favoring spontaneous wild germination. Growers frequently use humidity domes and propagation trays to establish a microclimate that promotes water absorption and lessens stress on newly emerged seedlings. Average temperatures, which fall between 72 and 78°F (22 and 26°C), encourage root development and metabolic activities. Whether artificial lighting with the right spectrum or natural sunlight, providing the right lighting conditions guarantees that seedlings get the energy they need for photosynthesis and early growth.

Maintaining healthy seedlings after successful germination requires close attention to post-germination care. Changing the environment to sustain continued growth is necessary during the shift from the germination stage to the vegetative stage. Propagation domes gradually lower their humidity levels so seedlings can acclimate to the surrounding humidity of the culture area. Seedlings are exposed to mild airflow to strengthen stems and prepare seedlings for the conditions they will face later in growth. Establishing a regular vegetative photoperiod, which involves 18-24 hours of light per day, can promote the development of a sturdy vegetative structure.

Proper irrigation is crucial in post-germination care, and growers must find a balance between giving plants enough moisture and not overwatering. Young seedlings are susceptible to fungal diseases like damping off, which can be a problem for seedlings that are especially sensitive to wet circumstances. Overwatering and promoting aeration of the root zone can be prevented by using a well-draining growth medium and letting the surface dry slightly in between waterings. Because seedlings are susceptible to chemicals and pH variations, the quality of the water utilized is essential. Providing seedlings with clean, pH-balanced water improves their general health.

There are few nutrient requirements at the seedling stage because seeds usually have enough nutrients to sustain early growth. However, producers may add a gentle and balanced nutrient solution to help seedlings adapt to the vegetative stage by providing necessary nutrients. Nutrient burns can be avoided by starting with a low concentration of nutrients, giving producers a better idea of how their seedlings will react. Many growers employ organic or specifically blended seedling fertilizers to guarantee a mild and suitable nutrition delivery throughout this critical stage.

A crucial stage in the development of seedlings is transplanting them into larger containers, which provide them the room and nutrients they require to keep growing. Seedlings with many sets of genuine leaves and a robust root system are usually ready for transplanting. The exact strain, the growing medium being used, and the intended eventual size of the plants all influence when to transplant. A smooth transition is ensured by using a growing medium that has been adequately prepared and by treating the seedlings with care during the transplanting process to reduce stress on them.

The growing media selection significantly impacts the health and growth of seedlings. Soil, soilless mixes, coco coir, and hydroponic systems are examples of standard growing media. Every medium has unique qualities, and growers choose their choices based on various criteria, including production objectives, personal preferences, and the particular requirements of the selected cannabis strains. Because of its inherent makeup and high nutritional content, soil is preferred for seedling growth. While hydroponic systems allow precise control over nutrient concentrations, soilless mixes and coco coir offer more control over nutrient delivery and aeration.

Lighting is essential for raising healthy seedlings, especially in the early phases of growth. Even while sunlight is a great source, many farmers utilize artificial lighting to provide even and controlled lighting. For seedlings, fluorescent lights are frequently used, especially ones with a spectrum that supports vegetative growth. Due to its tunable spectrum and energy economy, LED lights have become increasingly popular. A sufficient and steady supply of light is essential for photosynthesis, compact and robust growth, and the readiness of seedlings for the shift to the vegetative stage.

During the seedling stage, preventing stress is crucial since it can have long-lasting consequences on the general health and development of the plants. Environmental stressors include temperature swings, poor illumination, and sudden changes in humidity. Replanting and other seedling tasks should be handled carefully to reduce physical stress. Furthermore, nutritional stress is avoided by neither overfeeding nor giving too many nutrients, guaranteeing that seedlings receive the right amount of nutrition without experiencing negative consequences.

Seedling health is contingent upon regular observation and monitoring. The size, color, and general appearance of the leaves are examples of visual signals that offer essential information about the health of the seedlings. Based on these findings, changes can be made to the surrounding environment, irrigation techniques, or nutrient concentrations. During seedling, producers may occasionally encounter problems like pests, illnesses, or nutritional inadequacies. Plant development can be successfully mitigated, and possible setbacks can be avoided with early detection and timely management.

CHAPTER V

The Vegetative Stage

Managing Light Cycles

Controlling light cycles is an essential part of growing cannabis since it has a significant impact on the development and growth of the plants as well as the quality of the finished product. Photosynthesis, the process by which plants transform light energy into chemical energy and enable the synthesis of sugars and other necessary chemicals, is primarily driven by light. Growers can regulate the vegetative and blooming stages of cannabis development by adjusting the light cycles. This section examines the importance of controlling light cycles in cannabis production, reviewing the essential ideas, strategies, and factors that growers use to maximize plant productivity.

The vegetative and blooming stages are the two primary stages of a cannabis plant's life cycle. Specific light cycle needs for each stage are designed to replicate the natural circumstances found in the native habitats of these plants. Cannabis plants usually receive 18 to 24 hours of light daily during vegetative. This extended light exposure period promotes rapid vegetative growth, enabling the plants to create strong stems, robust leaves, and a vast root system.

When going from the vegetative stage to the blooming stage, when the focus switches from vegetative growth to the creation of flowers (buds), it is essential to lay a solid foundation. The length of the vegetative stage, which determines the growth and structure of the plants before triggering blooming, is controlled by cultivators by manipulating the light cycle. Whether to shorten or lengthen the vegetative light cycle depends on several variables, including the strains of cannabis that are selected, the amount of space that is available, and the goals of the growth.

To trigger flowering induction, the light cycle is changed to mimic the seasons, with fewer daylight hours indicating the arrival of fall. This change is accomplished in indoor culture by lowering the light cycle to a 12/12 schedule, alternating 12 hours of continuous light with 12 hours of darkness. The plants move from the vegetative to the blooming stage in response to this shift in the light cycle, which starts the formation of buds. Cultivators must carefully consider the timing of this shift since it affects how long the flowering stage lasts and, in turn, when the crop may be harvested.

Managing light cycles also heavily depends on light quality, including the light output spectrum. Cannabis plants use different light wavelengths for other physiological functions. The flowering stage benefits from a spectrum strong in red and orange light. In contrast, the vegetative stage benefits from a broader spectrum that includes blue light, encouraging compact development and healthy leaves. This shift in the spectrum encourages more significant, thicker buds to form throughout the flowering stage.

Thanks to developments in lighting technology, growers may now customize light cycles to suit their requirements. Indoor cannabis cultivation has historically relied on high-intensity discharge (HID) lights, such as metal halide (MH) for vegetative development and high-pressure sodium (HPS) for blooming. These lights offer a sufficient intensity and a well-balanced spectrum to assist plant growth throughout the cultivation cycle. Nevertheless, they have disadvantages, such as increased energy consumption and heat generation.

Light-emitting diode (LED) technology has become a more adaptable and energy-efficient solution to control light cycles. Cultivators can precisely adjust the light spectrum, intensity, and duration with LED lights. Growers can minimize energy use and heat output while creating ideal growing conditions for each stage of cannabis growth, thanks to this versatility. Moreover, LED lights are more affordable and environmentally friendly than conventional HID lights since they last longer and generate less heat.

Controlling light cycles involves more than just adjusting the length of day and night. Similar to numerous other plants, cannabis plants exhibit sensitivity to disruptions in the dark phase during the flowering cycle. Light pollution, also known as even brief exposure to light during the dark cycle, can interfere with a plant's biological processes and adversely affect the growth of its flowers. To preserve the integrity of the flowering stage, cultivators employ strategies like light-tight grow rooms, blackout curtains, or light deprivation systems that guarantee total darkness during the necessary dark phase.

Managing light cycles in outdoor horticulture brings with it unique opportunities and challenges. Although natural sunshine is a cheap and plentiful light source, adjusting to the changing seasons can be challenging. In response to the progressively fewer daylight hours in the fall, cannabis plants flower. To choose the best time to sow and harvest, outdoor farmers must consider the latitude, climate, and local weather. Furthermore, some cultivators manage or hasten the flowering process in outdoor environments by employing light deprivation techniques, such as covering plants to imitate darkness.

When fall approaches in areas with distinct seasons, cannabis plants may naturally experience fewer sunshine hours, indicating that blooming is about to commence. Yet, cannabis plants could need extra assistance to trigger flowering in equatorial areas where day length is comparatively constant all year round. In these areas, growers can imitate a dark phase by employing shade or light deprivation tactics, which will cause the plant to enter the flowering cycle.

Light cycles are essential for evaluating the general health, potency, and output of cannabis plants in addition to affecting their growth phases. Photosynthesis, which is necessary for the synthesis of terpenes, cannabinoids, and other secondary metabolites, as well as the synthesis of carbohydrates, depends on adequate light intensity, spectrum, and duration. Stretched, spindly plants with reduced yields and THC content can be the result of inadequate light. On the other hand, appropriate lighting conditions improve resin synthesis, potency, and the general quality of the harvested buds.

There is no one-size-fits-all method for controlling light cycles because different cannabis strains may react differently to different light levels. Certain strains have preferences or needs related to the delicate cycle, affecting things like blooming time, bud development, and general growth characteristics. Expert cultivators are acutely aware of the distinctive qualities of every strain and adjust their light cycle management strategy to suit the particular requirements and features of the plants they are growing.

Control and automation systems are now essential for controlling light cycles, particularly in industrial or large-scale cannabis farms. With the help of these devices, cultivators may precisely set and track light cycles, remotely modifying parameters like intensity, spectrum, and duration. Automated light control systems help maintain consistency, lower the possibility of human mistakes, and let growers design unique light schedules for various strains or growth objectives. Furthermore, these systems frequently interface with other environmental controls to produce a smooth and effective growing environment.

Beyond just maximizing plant growth and development, controlling light cycles is essential for resource efficiency and sustainability. Growing the cannabis business has led to many cultivators looking for ways to reduce energy use and environmental effects. LED technology supports these sustainability objectives because of its adjustable spectrum and energy economy. Furthermore, using light cycles that resemble natural circumstances lowers the requirement for excessive energy use and encourages ethical cultivation methods.

Nutrient Requirements

A vital component of cannabis growing, nutrient requirements are essential to the growth, development, and general health of the plant. Including all plants, cannabis depends on a wide range of vital nutrients for crucial physiological functions, including respiration, photosynthesis, and the production of essential chemicals like terpenes and cannabinoids. Producers must comprehend the unique nutrient requirements of cannabis plants at various growth stages to maximize yields, potency, and overall crop quality. This section examines the nutrients vital to cannabis, their functions in plant physiology, and the techniques growers use to guarantee sufficient and balanced nutrient delivery throughout the culture cycle.

There are two types of primary nutrients that cannabis needs: macronutrients and micronutrients. Plants require macronutrients in more significant quantities than micronutrients, which are necessary in lesser proportions. The macronutrients nitrogen (N), phosphorus (P), potassium (K), calcium (Ca), magnesium (Mg), and sulfur (S) are necessary for the production of cannabis. Each of these macronutrients contributes to a different component of plant growth and has a unique role in the physiology of cannabis.

Nitrogen is a vital component of chlorophyll, the pigment that absorbs light energy during photosynthesis. Growing robust stems, leaves and overall plant structure is essential. Cannabis plants need more nitrogen during the vegetative stage when strong growth and the development of a solid framework are prioritized. Cultivators typically use fertilizers designed for the vegetative stage to supply nitrogen, with the concentration of the fertilizer being adjusted according to the demands of the individual plants.

For plants to transfer energy, phosphorus is necessary. This is especially true for processes like photosynthesis and the production of nucleic acids. The growth of root systems, flowering, and general plant vigor depend on phosphorus. Throughout a cannabis plant's life, cultivators modify the amount of phosphorus in fertilizers to suit the plants' shifting needs. In particular, more phosphorus is needed during the flowering stage to assist the development of buds and flowers.

Potassium is essential for several physiological functions, such as the intake of water, the activation of enzymes, and the movement of nutrients throughout the plant. It helps cannabis plants endure environmental stressors like temperature swings and pest infestations by enhancing their general health and resilience. Since potassium supports several metabolic processes vital to plant development, adequate potassium levels are essential during a plant's life's vegetative and blooming stages.

A structural element of cell walls, calcium supports the integrity of individual cells as well as the overall structure of the plant. Additionally, calcium is involved in the intake and movement of nutrients within the plant. Throughout the culture cycle, it is critical to maintain an adequate calcium supply because it supports stem strength, root development, and the avoidance of diseases like blossom end rot in blooming plants.

Since magnesium is a critical component of the chlorophyll molecule, photosynthesis requires it. It also takes part in the intake of nutrients and energy transfer. A magnesium deficit can cause older leaves to turn yellow, negatively impacting the plant's capacity to absorb light energy. Cultivators often incorporate magnesium into fertilization regimens, particularly in the vegetative stage when there is a greater need for chlorophyll synthesis.

Another necessary component of proteins and amino acids, sulfur aids in creating several other molecules vital to plant growth. Younger leaves may become yellow as a result of a sulfur shortage. Sulfur is regularly replenished by cultivators, who also modify fertilizers to suit the unique requirements of cannabis plants at various phases of growth.

Cannabis plants also need micronutrients, albeit in smaller amounts than macronutrients. Iron (Fe), manganese (Mn), zinc (Zn), copper (Cu), boron (B), molybdenum (Mo), and chlorine (Cl) are examples of micronutrients. These micronutrients have a variety of functions in metabolism, enzyme activation, and general plant health.

Chlorophyll production and general energy transmission in plants depend on iron. Interveinal chlorosis, or yellowing between leaf veins, is a common sign of iron insufficiency. Cultivators often use chelated iron supplements or micronutrient fertilizers to alleviate iron deficiency.

Enzyme activation, nitrogen metabolism, and photosynthesis are all impacted by manganese. Symptoms of manganese deficiency include stunted development and yellowing between the veins on leaves. Growers modify their nutrient mixes so that cannabis plants receive enough manganese.

Zinc is essential for producing proteins and nucleic acids, hormone control, and activating enzymes involved in metabolic activities. A zinc deficit can cause deformed leaves and impaired growth. Zinc is frequently added to nutrient regimens by cultivators to alleviate possible inadequacies.

In addition to being necessary for activating enzymes, copper is involved in respiration and photosynthesis. A lack of copper can cause leaf discoloration and hinder plant growth. Cultivators closely monitor copper levels and modify fertilizers as needed to avoid deficits.

The synthesis of cell walls, pollination, and the metabolism of carbohydrates all depend on boron. A lack of boron can lead to stunted growth, less blooming, and poor seed formation. Growers add boron supplements as needed to keep cannabis plants at their ideal levels.

Enzyme activation and nitrogen metabolism are two processes in which molybdenum is involved. Symptoms of a molybdenum shortage include curling and yellowing of the leaves. Cultivators guarantee a balanced supply of molybdenum to support vital plant functions.

Chlorine is involved in photosynthesis and osmotic control, even though it is only needed in very minute amounts. Deficits in chlorine are uncommon because growing media and water frequently contain enough amounts of the mineral. When creating fertilizer solutions, cultivators consider the amount of chlorine present in water sources.

For cannabis growing, it's critical to attain the proper balance of nutrients, and growers frequently depend on fertilizers to supply the elements in the right amounts. Many different types of fertilizers are available, some of which are made especially for the vegetative or flowering stages. While some growers choose synthetic or mineral-based fertilizers for exact control over nutrient amounts, others prefer organic fertilizers from natural sources.

In hydroponic or soilless growth methods, cultivators frequently employ nutrient solutions, which deliver a liquid mixture of vital components straight to the plant's root zone. Deep water culture, nutrient film technology, and aeroponics are examples of popular hydroponic systems due to their effective nutrient uptake and ability to provide exact control over nutrient delivery. To ensure a balanced nutrient profile in soil-based cultivation, producers frequently amend the soil with organic matter or use potting mixes that have already been fertilized.

Pruning and Training Techniques

Techniques for training and pruning plants are crucial to cannabis production because they provide growers with efficient means of controlling plant development, increasing yields, and maximizing crop quality. These methods include carefully removing or modifying plant material to affect how energy is distributed, encouraging airflow, and regulating the structure of the plant. Cultivators utilize several strategies, ranging from simple pruning techniques to sophisticated training methods, to tailor the development patterns of their cannabis plants, with the ultimate goal of optimizing yield and strength.

A fundamental method of growing cannabis is pruning, which deliberately removes particular plant elements like leaves, branches, or buds. Keeping the plant's canopy in check so that light can reach the inner and lower branches of the plant is one of the main goals of pruning. Cultivators reduce the chance of moisture-related problems like mold and mildew by trimming off extra foliage, which leaves the canopy more open and well-ventilated. Furthermore, pruning promotes healthier and more rapid development by rerouting the plant's energy to critical growth zones.

When a plant is actively growing and establishing its structure, the pruning process starts during the vegetative stage. Fan leaves, or the more giant leaves that help shade the lower portions of the plant, are sometimes removed during pruning. Light can reach the lower branches and bud sites more easily when fan leaves are removed. Cultivators can also selectively prune to remove undesirable growth or focus energy on particular branches that are capable of robust development.

A common pruning technique is topping, which removes the plant's core or apical branch when it is still in its early vegetative stage. When a plant is topped, it develops several primary colas or prominent branches, which makes the plant structure bushier and more horizontally expansive. This method improves light distribution, stimulates lateral growth, and aids in the development of an even canopy. Increased branching and a more sturdy structure are common characteristics of topped plants, which help to increase yields when they flower.

Fimming is topping when only a piece of the apical shoot is removed instead of the complete tip. Cultivators pinch or cut off roughly 75% of the tip and encourage the remaining growth nodes to produce several shoots. More branching and lateral development might result from filming, a less exact process than topping. While topping yields two central colas, fimming can provide four or more shoots, which adds to the canopy's fullness.

Pruning during the blossoming stage is known as "lollipopping," which involves cutting off lower branches and foliage that get little light. The idea is to have a "lollipop" shape with minimal foliage below and a well-pruned upper canopy supported by a bare stem. Lollipopping directs the plant's energy toward the development and ripening of the higher buds, improves ventilation, and lowers the risk of pests and illnesses. This method works exceptionally well in indoor production settings where distributing light as efficiently as possible is essential.

Supercropping, often called high-stress training (HST), is a technique where a plant is purposefully stressed by bending or adjusting stems to induce a more horizontal growth pattern. The usual procedure is to squeeze or pinch the stems until they turn without breaking. Supercropping results in an equal canopy by promoting the formation of more secondary growth sites along the modified stems. This method works exceptionally well for controlling plant height and maximizing light exposure in small areas.

A more delicate method of controlling plant development is called low-stress training (LST), which involves carefully bending or tying down branches to make the canopy more level and open.

Usually applied in the vegetative stage, LST enables producers to direct the plant's growth without subjecting it to severe stress. Cultivators facilitate lateral growth and even dispersion of light by tying down branches and anchoring them to the growing media or support structure. LST is a valuable technique for raising yields and improving light utilization efficiency.

The Screen of Green (SCROG) training method uses a horizontal screen or net to direct and regulate plant development. The plants are positioned above the screen, and branches slowly weave through the holes in the screen as they develop. This technique exposes several bud locations to direct light and guarantees an equal canopy. SCROG is incredibly well-liked in indoor production, where cultivators aim to maximize space utilization and establish a consistent, adequate canopy. This method works with a variety of cannabis strains and can be adjusted to fit different growing conditions.

A sophisticated training method called mainlining, or manifold training, entails forming the plant into a symmetrical, well-structured form. The technique starts with topping or filming during the early vegetative stage to produce many central colas. As the plant grows, certain branches are clipped off as needed, leaving just a few strategically placed branches that create a symmetrical pattern. Mainlining aims to produce a more regulated and orderly plant structure while optimizing the potential of each main cola. This method can produce higher yields and a visually pleasing plant architecture, but it does require careful design and execution.

Although there are many advantages to pruning and training methods, growers must handle these procedures carefully and consider the unique requirements and traits of every cannabis variety. Excessive trimming or improper training methods can cause stress, lower yields, or stunted development. Furthermore, the timing of these

Methods are essential, and to use pruning and training successfully, cultivators need to be aware of the stage at which their plants are growing. In summary, cannabis growers' toolkit is incomplete without pruning and training procedures, which offer methods for directing plant growth, increasing yields, and maximizing crop quality overall. Cultivators have a variety of options to tailor the growth patterns of their cannabis plants, ranging from simple pruning during the vegetative stage to more complex training techniques like SCROG and mainlining. To apply these procedures with caution, one must be aware of the unique requirements of each strain and maintain flexibility and close monitoring throughout the cultivation cycle. Cultivators will hone and develop their pruning and training techniques as the cannabis business grows, opening new avenues for increased productivity and harvesting success.

CHAPTER VI

Flowering and Bud Development

Transitioning to the Flowering Stage

When cannabis plants enter the flowering stage, it is a significant turning point in their life cycle, one in which the emphasis moves from vegetative growth to the formation of flowers and, eventually, potent buds. Cultivators who aim to optimize crop quality, potency, and yields must comprehend the crucial components of this meticulously planned procedure. During the flowering stage, the cannabis plant experiences a fantastic metamorphosis from a lush, green structure to an abundance of resin-coated buds, each of which has the potential to contain a wide variety of terpenes and cannabinoids.

The quick growth and formation of a strong plant structure that characterizes the vegetative phase is the first step toward the flowering stage. During this phase, cultivators take great care to tend to their plants, ensuring they have the right light, nutrients, and environmental conditions to support rapid growth. A crucial factor to consider is the length of the vegetative phase, which establishes the plant's growth and structure before flowering. Cultivators carefully schedule this transition to maximize the next flowering stage and attain the ideal plant size.

Changing the light cycle is one of the leading causes of the change to the flowering stage. With its shorter days, fall is heralded by the shifting of the seasons in nature. In response to these environmental cues, cannabis plants begin to blossom as a survival strategy, focusing their energy on producing flowers and seeds.

Replicating this natural process in indoor culture entails modifying the light cycle during blooming from a more extended golden period—typically 18 to 24 hours per day —to a 12/12 light-dark cycle. This change in the delicate cycle causes the plant to refocus on its reproductive processes to correspond with the seasonal changes.

For growers, choosing when to start the flowering stage is crucial. It is influenced by several variables, such as the type of cannabis being grown, the size of the intended plants, and the overall objectives of the growth process. While some cultivators choose a more extended vegetative stage to produce more significant structures, others may prefer a shorter vegetative phase to retain smaller plants. Furthermore, because of their quick development and relatively small size, auto-flowering strains—which have a predetermined flowering period independent of light cycles—have become increasingly popular.

Physiological changes occur as the cannabis plant moves into the flowering stage. Pre-flowers, tiny structures that reveal the plant's gender and hint at the upcoming growth of buds, are some of the most noticeable changes. While female plants develop pistils, which resemble hairs and collect pollen for seed formation, male plants generate pollen sacs. To avoid unwanted pollination, cultivators take great care to identify and segregate the male plants, concentrating their efforts on supporting the female plants to yield the resinous blooms consumers wish to consume.

Buds develop quickly during the early blooming stage, which is also marked by an increase in resin production and the appearance of aromatic terpenes. Cultivators maintain a balanced nutrition regimen at this stage, modifying formulas to suit the plants' evolving requirements. Phosphorus, in particular, becomes essential since it helps buds develop overall and facilitates the creation of flowers.

Cultivators can use bloom-specific fertilizers to ensure the nutrient profile meets the plant's needs during the flowering stage.

An essential aspect of the blossoming stage's success is the environment. The plant switches its attention from vegetative growth to floral formation, at which point temperature, humidity, and airflow become crucial factors. Sustaining ideal conditions aids in avoiding problems like mildew or mold, which can be especially troublesome when the buds are closely spaced during the blossoming stage. It becomes essential to have enough ventilation and air circulation to reduce the likelihood of pests and illnesses while encouraging healthy bud development.

Growers frequently adjust environmental factors in indoor cultivation to get the perfect flowering environment. An environment favorable to healthy bud growth is created by keeping temperature and humidity levels within a specific range, usually between 68-78°F (20-26°C) and 40-60% humidity. Furthermore, consistent airflow is maintained by appropriate ventilation and fan use, which lowers the possibility of moisture-related problems and guarantees that fresh air is distributed evenly throughout the plant.

The light spectrum that cannabis plants need varies as they go from the vegetative to the blooming stage. Plants benefit from a broader spectrum of light, with higher amounts of blue light, during the vegetative stage. But a spectrum rich in red and orange light becomes crucial to produce dense, resinous buds during the flowering period. When using artificial lighting systems like light-emitting diode (LED) or high-pressure sodium (HPS) lamps, growers frequently modify the color spectrum to meet the unique requirements of the flowering stage.

Cultivators carefully monitor the buds' growth as the flowering stage advances, noting characteristics including bud size, density, and resin production.

One vital sign that a crop is ready for harvesting is the presence of microscopic resin glands called trichomes on the surface of the buds. As the cannabinoids within the buds mature, trichomes change from clear to hazy and finally amber. Cultivators must carefully consider when to harvest because it affects the ultimate product's potency, flavor, and general quality.

Before harvesting, growers frequently impose a dark

period in the later stages of the flowering phase, also referred to as the flush or flush-out period. This method denies the plants light for a predetermined time, usually a few days to a week. Through the use of stored nutrients and the prevention of residual salts building up in the buds, the flush is thought to improve the quality of the finished crop. Cultivators carefully adjust the flush length to get the best results without stressing the plants.

Since plants grown outside are subject to ambient conditions and sunlight during the blossoming stage, further considerations must be made. Cultivators must be aware of variations in local climate patterns, such as day length, temperature, and humidity. Cannabis plants in areas with various seasons automatically go into flowering when the number of daylight hours decreases. Cultivators may need to use methods such as light deprivation or shading in equatorial regions where day length is constant, mainly to stimulate flowering.

In addition to experiencing rapid bud development, the

flowering stage is marked by increased resin production, which triggers the synthesis of terpenes and cannabinoids. These substances influence aspects like flavor, fragrance, and overall impacts of cannabis in addition to its medicinal and psychotropic qualities. The variety of strains that are accessible in The complex interactions between genetics and environmental factors throughout the flowering stage give rise to a variety of rare and sought-after cultivars, which are reflected in the cannabis market.

Bud Formation and Growth

Creating highly sought-after flowering structures results from careful attention to detail and calculated decisions made during the vegetative and flowering stages of cannabis production. Bud's formation and growth mark the culmination of this trip. The core of the medicinal and intoxicating qualities of the cannabis plant is contained in these resin-coated buds, which have a rich tapestry of terpenes and cannabinoids. Growers must comprehend bud creation and growth nuances to attain the best possible yields, potency, and overall crop quality.

The shift to the flowering stage, brought on by modifications in the light cycle, marks the beginning of the process leading to bud production. The plant senses a decrease in daylight hours and directs its energy from growth into vegetative blooms, preparing the way for the formation of buds. Pre-flowers are tiny, teardrop-shaped structures that appear as the first indications of bud initiation. The gender of the plant is indicated by these pre-flowers, where males display pollen sacs, and females show pistils, hair-like structures that collect pollen for seed formation. To stop unintentional pollination, cultivators carefully locate and eliminate male plants, allowing the female plants to concentrate on developing seedless, resinous buds.

The pre-flowers turn into densely packed clusters of buds that hold the potential to release a wide variety of terpenes and cannabinoids as the blooming stage advances. Bud development follows a pattern where buds emerge at the nodes, usually where leaves and branches join, rather than being uniform throughout the plant. The top frequently produces more significant, more robust buds, more direct-lit areas of the plant, while the lower, less exposed sections may produce smaller, less dense buds. Cultivators use pruning and training strategies during the vegetative stage to generate an equal canopy and maximize light exposure to all bud locations because of this natural variability.

A cannabis bud's anatomy is a marvel of nature, made up of various parts that work together to give it structure and potency. Trichomes are small resin glands that coat the buds' surface and are essential to the production and build-up of terpenes and cannabinoids. In addition to providing the plant with defense against external stresses and possible predators, these resinous structures act as the central repositories of the bioactive substances consumers are interested in. A crucial clue that a bud is ready for harvesting is the development of its trichomes, which alter in size, color, and shape to indicate when to harvest for the best results.

Cannabinoids and terpenes work together within the bud to produce the distinct chemical profile that characterizes a given strain. Two well-known cannabinoids that provide unique medicinal and psychoactive qualities to the overall cannabis experience are tetrahydrocannabinol (THC) and cannabidiol (CBD). Terpenes are aromatic molecules present in many different plants, including cannabis. Terpenes give buds a wide range of smells and fragrances. The entourage effect, a complex interaction between terpenes and cannabinoids, affects a cannabis strain's overall effects and possible advantages.

During the flowering stage, cultivators anxious to maximize the production of terpenes and cannabinoids pay close attention to environmental conditions, fertilizer regimes, and farming procedures. The production of terpenes and cannabinoids is aided by appropriate nutrient management, especially regarding the availability of potassium and phosphorus. Rich in nutrients, soil, or carefully mixed hydroponic solutions improve the plant's general health and capacity to develop potent buds. The precise selection of cannabis strains, each with a distinct genetic profile, is also essential in establishing the properties and chemical makeup of the final buds.

Environmental factors, including temperature, humidity, and airflow, significantly influence the creation and growth of buds. The best conditions for resin production are fostered by keeping an environment that is stable and controlled, avoiding problems like mold or mildew that can lower the quality of the buds. Ventilation becomes essential to maintain enough air circulation and reduce the danger of pests or illnesses. Adjusting environmental parameters is especially important for indoor cultivation because growers have more control over the growth environment there.

Lighting concerns further influence bud formation during the flowering stage. High-intensity discharge (HID) lights, like metal halide (MH) or high-pressure sodium (HPS), have been standard equipment in indoor production for a long time because they can produce the intensity and spectrum needed for strong bud growth. On the other hand, light-emitting diode (LED) technology has completely changed the market by enabling growers to achieve more precise lighting parameters for certain strains or production objectives, increased energy efficiency, and spectrum customization. The plant will receive the ideal wavelengths for photosynthesis, resin production, and general bud growth if the light spectrum is adjusted to suit the requirements of the flowering stage.

Different cannabis strains have other flowering times, but they usually last between six and twelve weeks. Growers keep an eye on the development of buds by routinely examining the color and shape of the trichomes. The transition of trichomes from clear to hazy and finally amber indicates that the buds' cannabinoids are maturing. Harvesting cannabis at the right time of year requires careful consideration of many aspects, including flavor, strength, and consumer preferences. While harvesting too late can result in higher THC breakdown and a more soothing effect, harvesting too early can produce buds that are less mature and potent.

The procedures carried out after harvest are essential to maintaining the quality of buds and getting them ready for ingestion. Drying and curing are two crucial processes that enhance taste and fragrance development and the overall smoking or vaping experience. To keep terpenes and cannabinoids intact while avoiding mold or mildew, the buds must be thoroughly dried. The more protracted process of "curing" involves keeping dried buds under carefully monitored circumstances so that any residual moisture may be released gradually and the desired tastes and fragrances can develop. Buds that have been appropriately cured and dried have more potency, smoother combustion, and a more enjoyable smoking experience.

Growth and development of buds. Cutting-edge growing techniques, including aquaponics, aeroponics, and hydroponics, provide exact control over fertilizer delivery and accelerate nutrient uptake. When combined with ideal climatic conditions, these technologies lead to faster growth and larger yields. Furthermore, cutting-edge methods like tissue culture and genetic engineering show promise for creating novel cultivars with certain qualities that might completely alter the cannabis market.

To sum up, bud creation and growth are the pinnacle of the cannabis growing process when the science and art of cultivation come together to yield the resinous blossoms that both patients and enthusiasts want. Every stage of bud growth, from the beginning of pre-flowers to the formation of trichomes, is evidence of the meticulous attention to detail and calculated choices made by cultivators. The complex interactions between genetics, environment, and growing techniques throughout the flowering stage determine the product's chemical makeup, aroma, and effects. Cultivators will surely push the envelope of innovation as the cannabis market develops, opening up new avenues for improved bud quality and customer pleasure.

Monitoring and Adjusting Environmental Factors

Effective cannabis growing relies heavily on monitoring and modifying environmental parameters, which are a dynamic interplay between the demands of the plant and its surroundings. To establish the ideal growth environment for cannabis plants, cultivators must carefully control various environmental factors, whether in a greenhouse, outside, or indoors. Every element that affects the plants' general health, development, and potency—from temperature and humidity to light intensity and air circulation—contributes. This section highlights cultivators' complex techniques to create an environment that supports robust plant development and high-quality yields. It also examines the vital importance of monitoring and adjusting these environmental factors throughout the various stages of cannabis cultivation.

One of the central tenets of environmental management in cannabis cultivation is temperature regulation. Throughout their life cycle, cannabis plants show specific preferences for different temperatures. Temperatures in the 70–85°F (21–29°C) are optimum for vegetative growth because they encourage rapid growth and maximum metabolic activity. Cultivators frequently slightly lower temperatures as plants approach the flowering stage to maximize resin production and terpene synthesis. However, it is crucial to keep the temperature steady because variations can cause stress to the plants, affect how well they absorb nutrients, and even result inunfavorable effects like hermaphroditism.

HVAC (heating, ventilation, and air conditioning) systems are used in indoor horticulture to achieve exact temperature control. By preserving a constant temperature inside the growing area, these devices lessen the impact of outside influences. Insulation and reflecting materials are also used to control heat dispersion and guarantee a consistent temperature gradient across the canopy. Cultivators that work outside depend on the weather, but they can also use strategies like shade or timing plantings to maximize local temperature conditions.

In the hierarchy of environmental elements impacting cannabis cultivation, humidity levels follow temperature closely. Higher humidity levels, between 40 and 70 percent, generally benefit the vegetative stage as they promote strong growth and avoid dehydration. But humidity must be reduced to reduce the chance of mold and mildew during the blossoming stage—especially in the closely spaced buds. Cultivators deliberately control humidity through thoughtful watering techniques, dehumidifiers, and ventilation. Exhaust fans and well-designed ventilation systems promote proper air circulation, which helps retain moisture and keeps out stagnant air, which can exacerbate humidity-related problems.

A key component in growing cannabis is lighting, which needs to be carefully monitored and adjusted to meet the needs of the plant for photosynthetic processes. Indoor growers use artificial lighting systems, including metal halide (MH), high-pressure sodium (HPS), or light-emitting diode (LED) lights, to provide the spectrum and intensity needed for healthy growth. While the flowering stage requires a spectrum strong in red and orange wavelengths to stimulate bud development, the vegetative stage benefits from a broader spectrum that contains more blue light. To replicate the variations in the natural photoperiod, cultivators deliberately modify the light cycle, moving from a more extended day during the vegetative stage to a 12/12 light-dark cycle during flowering.

Natural sunshine is necessary for outdoor production, and growers frequently select strains appropriate for the local environment and photoperiod. However, light availability can be impacted by external factors like cloudy days or seasonal variations. To counteract these effects, growers can adjust the photoperiod by using soft deprivation techniques or additional illumination to ensure plants get the right light for strong bud formation and healthy growth.

In cannabis growing, air circulation is an important yet sometimes disregarded environmental component. Static air is avoided, gas exchange is facilitated, and plant structures are strengthened by healthy air movement. In indoor gardening, oscillating fans and exhaust systems are positioned carefully to encourage airflow, avoid moisture accumulation, and fortify plant stems. Proper air circulation is essential in highly populated grow rooms, where it helps reduce the risk of pests, illnesses, and temperature variations over the canopy.

Cultivators also monitor and modify the amounts of carbon dioxide (CO_2) to maximize plant growth. Cannabis plants benefit from high CO_2 levels throughout the vegetative stage, usually between 800 and 1,500 parts per million (ppm). Because of this supplementation, photosynthesis is improved, resulting in faster growth and more biomass. As carbon dioxide needs to fall during the flowering stage, ambient CO_2 levels are frequently maintained. Indoor culture uses CO_2 enrichment equipment, such as tanks or generators, to maintain ideal levels and encourage rapid vegetative development.

Nutrient availability in the growing medium must be continuously monitored to maintain a balanced and nourishing substrate, as it is closely linked to environmental conditions. Both soil and soilless media require careful management of nutrient concentrations, which is a skill that cultivators possess. Whereas hydroponic or soilless growers use fertilizer solutions, soil-based cultivators may use pre-fertilized potting mixes or modify their medium with organic matter. The availability of nutrients to plants is influenced by pH; hence, checking pH levels regularly is essential. Cultivators carefully regulate pH levels to guarantee the best possible nutrient uptake and avoid deficiencies or toxicities that may result from growth media imbalances.

A critical factor in cannabis growing is water quality. Therefore, growers must be careful to watch for any pollutants or pH or nutritional imbalances in their water sources. Different amounts of minerals, chlorine, or other contaminants in tap, well, or municipal water can impact the health of plants. Before utilizing water for irrigation, cultivators frequently use water filtering equipment or let the water lie in the open to release chlorine.

Geographical location, seasonal variations, and the innate unpredictability of natural conditions all affect environmental parameters, which are never constant. Cultivators need to modify their approaches to handle these dynamic changes and maintain an optimal growing environment. For best results during flowering, outdoor cultivators in regions with distinct seasons might adjust planting schedules to match the natural photoperiod. Growers in greenhouses utilize. Utilizing climate control systems, one can create a hybrid environment that incorporates indoor and outdoor production advantages by adjusting temperature, humidity, and light levels.

Integrating pest management (IPM) aims to avoid and mitigate pest and disease problems with a proactive approach to environmental elements. Utilizing a blend of biological, chemical, and cultural techniques, cultivators create an environment that is hostile to pests and encourages beneficial species that serve as natural predators. A comprehensive IPM plan includes employing biological controls, such as predatory insects, employing pest-resistant strains, and keeping a growing area tidy and orderly.

CHAPTER VII

Pest and Disease Management

Identifying Common Pests

It is a difficulty that has been there for a very long time and requires our attention and devotion because pests exist in our living and working environments. In addition to causing damage to property and spreading diseases, pests can also compromise the overall well-being of persons. Pests can cause havoc in various settings, including houses and agricultural fields. One of the most critical steps in efficient pest management and prevention is the identification of these common pests. In the following paragraphs, we will delve into the wide-ranging realm of pests, examining the traits, habits, and potential dangers of some of the most common pests.

A Wide Variety of Unwanted Insects Regarding the category of pests, insects are at the top of the list because they are among the most annoying and pervasive offenders. Ants, for example, are omnipresent pests that establish colonies in various habitats, searching for food sources and leaving behind distinctive trails. On the other hand, termites are silent destroyers that cause structural damage to buildings and wooden structures. Termites are responsible for this destruction. As a result of their flexibility and tenacity, cockroaches are not only an annoyance, but they also threaten human health since they carry contagious diseases. Even though they are tiny, bed bugs are infamous for their ability to infest bedding and furnishings, which can lead to discomfort and allergic reactions.

Rats and mice are a nuisance that can have far-reaching consequences. They are infamous for their ability to penetrate human homes, where they can cause harm and spread diseases. Rodents, such as rats and mice, are examples of rodents. Rats, in particular, are adept climbers and can squeeze through shockingly small gaps. They can chew through wiring, insulation, and even structural components if they have gained access to the building, which might result in serious fire concerns. Furthermore, rodents are carriers of various diseases, including leptospirosis and hantavirus, making their presence a significant health risk that requires quick attention.

Weaving Webs of Exploitation: The Role of Arachnids

Arachnids, which include ticks and spiders, are another type of pest that has the potential to cause significant distress. Some spiders, such as the black widow or the brown recluse, can produce venom and pose a risk to human beings. However, most spiders are harmless and even helpful in suppressing other pests. Because ticks, frequently discovered in outdoor settings, are vectors for diseases such as Lyme, it is essential to identify and remove ticks to prevent the widespread transmission of infections.

The Green Intruders That Are Invasive Plants Invasive

plants can also threaten ecosystems and human activities in essential ways. Pests are not restricted to the animal kingdom; they can also be found in the plant kingdom. For instance, weeds such as Japanese knotweed and kudzu have the potential to spread rapidly, which can result in the displacement of native vegetation and the creation of ecological imbalances. In the field of agriculture, invasive plants compete with crops for resources, which results in decreased yields and has an effect on the production of food. Identifying these invasive species is essential to implementing efficient control methods that will reduce their harmful consequences.

The Threat That Is Not Visible: Microorganisms Pests that

are caused by microorganisms, such as bacteria, viruses, and fungi, can be highly hazardous to human health, agricultural production, and the environment as a whole.

Salmonella and E. coli are two examples of pathogenic bacteria that have the potential to contaminate food and water, giving rise to widespread sickness. The Zika virus, which is spread by mosquitoes, is one example of a virus that can cause epidemics with far-reaching implications. Mold is one example of a fungal pest that not only causes damage to structures and materials but also contributes to respiratory problems associated with humans.

Integrated Pest Management: An Approach Utilizing Holistic Methods. The identification of common pests is only the first stage in the process of effective pest management. Integrated Pest Management (IPM) is a concept that emphasizes using a holistic and environmentally responsible approach to managing pests. Biological control, cultural practices, and pharmaceutical interventions are some of the tactics utilized in this method, which is a blend of different approaches. Individuals can apply targeted actions that minimize the use of toxic pesticides and create a healthier environment if they are aware of pests' life cycles and behaviors.

The most critical aspects of effective pest management are prevention and early detection. Unlike dealing with problems already created, preventing insect infestations is typically more controllable. Essential preventative actions include performing routine maintenance, appropriately managing trash, and closing entry points. When pest problems are identified and addressed in their early phases, it is possible to prevent widespread infestations and reduce the required extensive interventions. Early identification is equally important. Maintaining vigilance and conducting routine inspections are essential components of a proactive approach that helps limit the hazards connected with common pests.

Final Thoughts. In conclusion, when it comes to preserving healthy and pest-free settings, one of the most important aspects is the identification of common pests. Pests come in various forms, including insects, rodents, arachnids, invasive plants, and microbiological threats.

The world of pests is multifaceted and ever-changing. Effective pest control requires several critical components, including recognizing the indicators of infestations and comprehending the behavior of undesirable organisms. Individuals and communities can protect their homes, crops, and well-being from the ubiquitous issues posed by common pests by taking a comprehensive approach, combining preventative measures, and implementing solutions for integrated pest management. Knowledge and preventive actions become vital in preserving a balanced and pest-free environment in a world where coexistence with pests is unavoidable.

Implementing Organic Pest Control Methods

The growing interest in organic pest management techniques corresponds with the desire for healthy living and environmental sustainability. Using natural, non-toxic options to manage and lessen pest-related problems is known as organic pest control. Several accessible organic pest control techniques will be discussed in this section, along with their advantages, efficacy, and significance in household pest management, gardening, and agriculture.

Using the ability of natural predators to control pest populations, biological control is one of the central tenets of organic pest management. Aphids and caterpillars target beneficial insects like ladybugs, lacewings, and predatory beetles, which are prey for destructive pests. This strategy reduces the need for chemical interventions, which may have negative environmental impacts, making it both sustainable and effective. Biological management improves biodiversity and upholds the environment's natural checks and balances by encouraging a balanced ecosystem.

A tried-and-true organic pest control technique called companion planting entails planting various crops strategically next to one another to promote mutual growth and discourage pests. Some plants emit natural substances that serve as a natural barrier by repelling particular pests. For instance, placing basil next to tomatoes will deter aphids, while growing marigolds beside tomatoes can aid in nematode resistance. By protecting crops and promoting a more robust and varied ecology, this harmonic strategy lessens the need for artificial pesticides.

Neem oil, which comes from the seeds of the neem tree, is a popular and adaptable organic pest management solution. It has ingredients that interfere with the life cycles of several pests, such as fungi and insects. Neem oil is an invaluable tool for farmers and gardeners, as it functions as a natural fungicide, pesticide, and miticide. Neem oil's organic and environmentally friendly qualities are further highlighted by the fact that helpful insects like bees and butterflies find it reasonably safe to use.

Diatomaceous earth is a fine powder made from fossilized diatoms, which are microscopic algae with silica skeletons. Diatomaceous earth functions as a desiccant when applied to soil or plants directly, which causes exoskeleton-containing insects like ants, fleas, and beetles to get dehydrated and eventually die. Since diatomaceous earth is non-toxic to people and animals, unlike chemical pesticides, it is a safe yet efficient option for controlling organic pests. It is a well-liked choice for individuals looking for sustainable solutions due to its long-lasting effects and small environmental footprint.

A key component of organic farming is crop rotation, which entails changing the kinds of crops planted in particular fields each growing season. By upsetting the life cycles of pests unique to specific crops, this technique keeps them from becoming established long-term residents. Farmers who rotate their crops reduce the accumulation of pests and illnesses carried by the soil, resulting in healthier soil and higher crop yields without chemical treatments. Crop rotation fits perfectly with the precepts of organic agriculture as a comprehensive and preventative strategy.

Trap crops are yet another tactical method for organic pest management. This entails growing particular crops that serve as decoys, drawing pests away from the primary crops. Pests can be more readily controlled or eliminated without seriously harming the main crops once they are attracted to the trap crops. Aphids, for example, can be deterred from attacking more valuable crops by using mustard greens as a trap crop. This focused approach maintains the ecosystem's general health by reducing the need for broad-spectrum insecticides.

A common strategy for organic pest management is to use everyday household products to develop quick yet efficient treatments. Mix everyday items like soap, garlic, and chili peppers to make DIY insecticidal sprays. These mixtures prevent or interfere with the feeding and reproduction of pests. Despite their lack of potency, these natural solutions for small-scale pest control, especially in home gardens, are an affordable and eco-friendly alternative to synthetic poisons.

Although using organic pest management techniques has many advantages, there are also drawbacks. The possibility of a slower rate of efficacy in comparison to chemical pesticides is an essential factor. Organic treatments frequently take longer; you might need to use them again to get the desired effects. Furthermore, weather conditions like heavy rain might wash away organic pesticides, necessitating constant monitoring and reapplication.

A change in perspective and behavior is necessary to use organic pest management approaches, emphasizing awareness and education. Information regarding the advantages of organic farming practices, appropriate application methods, and the significance of long-term sustainability should be easily accessible to farmers, gardeners, and homeowners. Outreach campaigns, training courses, and workshops are essential in promoting a general awareness of the benefits and effectiveness of organic pest control.

In summary, employing organic pest management techniques is a sustainable and eco-friendly way to control pests in homes, gardens, and agricultural settings. A wide range of organic options are available, including companion planting, biological control, neem oil, diatomaceous earth, crop rotation, trap crops, and home cures. Adopting these practices promotes a more positive and harmonious interaction between humans and the environment while reducing the detrimental effects of synthetic chemicals on ecosystems. Organic solutions as we negotiate pest management challenges are evidence of our dedication to protecting the environment for the coming generations.

Disease Prevention and Treatment

The foundations of public health, which influence people's and communities' wellbeing globally, are disease prevention and treatment. The complex interactions between genetics, lifestyle, and environment highlight the intricacy of disease dynamics. This section will examine the various approaches used in illness prevention and treatment, highlighting the significance of a comprehensive strategy that includes preventative actions and successful interventions.

A healthy society is built on prevention, which includes a variety of tactics meant to lower the prevalence of illness. One of the most critical developments in preventive medicine has been vaccination programs, which have been instrumental in halting the spread of infectious diseases. Vaccines against measles and polio prevent severe illnesses and build population immunity. In addition to immunizations, health education and promotion initiatives allow people to make knowledgeable lifestyle decisions and encourage practices that improve general health.

The proverb "prevention is better than cure" has a strong resonance in public health. Making lifestyle changes, such as eating well, exercising frequently, and managing stress, is essential to preventing chronic illnesses like obesity, diabetes, and cardiovascular disease. Regular physical exercise combined with a well-balanced diet high in fruits, vegetables, and whole grains creates a powerful barrier against various health problems. Because lifestyle interventions have a long-term effect of lowering the burden of preventable diseases, governments, and healthcare providers worldwide are increasingly emphasizing the relevance of these treatments more and more.

Environmental factors significantly shape the consequences of public health. Respiratory disorders, allergies, and some types of cancer can be more common due to pollution, poor air quality, and exposure to dangerous substances. Preserving the environment is just as crucial as making personal decisions when preventing disease. A better living environment is facilitated by policies that manage trash, encourage sustainable behaviors, and lessen air and water pollution. Communities that promote longevity and wellbeing must address environmental determinants of health.

An essential component of efficient illness management is early detection. Healthcare providers can detect possible health problems before symptoms appear with routine screens and diagnostic testing, allowing prompt intervention. For instance, cancer screenings help identify cancers at earlier, more manageable stages of the disease. A proactive approach to healthcare involves routine check-ups, blood tests, and imaging treatments to prevent diseases from developing to advanced and often more difficult-to-treat stages.

Strong control measures are essential given the persistent threats that infectious illnesses represent to the world community. The advent of new viruses, like the SARS-CoV-2 virus that caused the COVID-19 pandemic, emphasizes the importance of efficient surveillance, quick reaction mechanisms, and worldwide cooperation. Campaigns for vaccination, travel restrictions, and quarantine policies are essential strategies in the fight against infectious disease transmission. Global initiatives to improve vaccine accessibility, strengthen healthcare infrastructure, and promote information exchange are critical to the continuous battle against new disease threats.

Although illness prevention creates the foundation for a healthier society, diseases will inevitably arise. The efficacy of treatment techniques assumes significant importance in tackling current health issues. Many different treatment options are available, ranging from pharmaceutical treatments to surgical operations and rehabilitative therapies, thanks to advancements in medical research and technology.

The introduction of medications and vaccines, among other pharmaceutical interventions, has completely changed how diseases are treated. Antibiotics, for instance, have prevented bacterial infections and saved many lives. The global effort to create COVID-19 vaccines is an example of how necessary vaccinations are in averting serious illnesses and lessening the impact of infectious diseases on people. Better treatment outcomes and better patient care are potential benefits of ongoing research and development of new pharmaceuticals.

Surgical interventions have developed into complex processes that cover a wide range of illnesses. To cure disorders that call for accuracy and structural rectification, surgical interventions—from simple surgeries like appendectomies to intricate organ transplants and minimally invasive procedures—are essential. Technological developments, such as robotically assisted surgeries, improve patient outcomes by improving surgical precision and safety.

Treatment for diseases must include rehabilitation therapy, particularly for those suffering from operations, trauma, or long-term illnesses. The goals of speech-language pathology, physical therapy, and occupational therapy are to improve mobility, restore function, and raise general quality of life. These treatments support patients' holistic care by addressing the long-term effects on daily functioning, overall wellbeing, and the acute health problem.

In recent years, there has been an increased awareness of the importance of mental health to total well-being. Comprehensive treatment approaches are necessary for a variety of mental health illnesses, ranging from mild conditions like depression and anxiety to more severe ones like schizophrenia. To address mental health issues, pharmaceutical therapies, psychotherapy, and counseling are essential. Incorporating mental health assistance into overall healthcare frameworks is crucial to promoting a patient-centered and holistic approach to illness treatment.

There are obstacles and moral dilemmas in illness prevention and treatment. Socioeconomic gaps, healthcare access, and the ethical implications of new medical technologies raise complex concerns. Managing health disparities, guaranteeing fair access to healthcare, and managing the moral ramifications of developing biotechnologies are persistent difficulties that require cooperation from governments, healthcare professionals, and the general public.

In summary, the prevention and treatment of disease are complex and interrelated aspects of public health that influence people's quality of life individually and collectively. A comprehensive strategy is necessary, encompassing everything from lifestyle changes, vaccines, and environmental health to pharmaceutical interventions, surgery, and rehabilitative therapy as therapeutic options. The complexity of the profession is highlighted by the persistent problems with newly emerging infectious diseases, the requirement for fair access to healthcare, and the ethical questions raised by medical developments. Building resilient and healthy societies requires a commitment to holistic and patient-centered methods as we navigate the constantly changing healthcare landscape.

CHAPTER VIII

Harvesting and Drying

Determining the Right Time to Harvest

In agriculture, harvesting is a crucial event that marks the end of weeks or months of careful upkeep and development. The optimal time to harvest is a difficult choice that requires careful balancing between several variables, such as market demands, plant maturity, and weather. In this section, we shall examine several factors that farmers must consider to determine the best time to harvest their crops. Harvest time is closely linked to the entire process, from the science of plant maturation to the effects of environmental factors and market dynamics.

Determining the ideal time to harvest crops requires

understanding the physiological processes that control plant development. From germination to maturity, plants undergo a succession of phases, each distinguished by distinct growth and reproductive benchmarks. One of the most significant markers of the ideal harvest period is frequently the maturity of the plant's reproductive organs, such as seeds or fruits. For instance, color shifts, texture, and sugar content in fruits like tomatoes or apples are good markers of ripeness. When assessing when a grain is ready for harvest, it is essential to pay attention to the color and firmness of the kernels, particularly in wheat or rice. The complex interactions between genetic variables, environmental cues, and plant hormones impact these processes, so farmers need to become well-versed in the distinctive qualities of each crop.

Environmental considerations play a significant role in determining the ideal time to harvest. Climate factors such as temperature, humidity, and precipitation can affect crop quality and yield. For instance, excessive rainfall can lead to soggy soil and negatively impact the health of the roots, making it difficult to harvest some crops. Conversely, dry conditions accelerate the maturation process and necessitate an early harvest. Farmers must carefully time their harvest to avoid damage from frost, which can harm delicate crops. Moreover, variations in ambient temperature and sunshine exposure can influence the taste, color, and nutritional value of fruits and vegetables. Due to the intricate relationship between climate and weather, farmers must regularly monitor forecasts and adjust their harvest timetables accordingly.

The circumstances in the field are not the only factors that influence when to harvest; post-harvest processing and storage are also important factors. In crops meant for eating right away, like fresh produce, the key is to pick them at their ripest to guarantee the best possible flavor and nutritional value. On the other hand, crops like grains or tubers meant to be processed or stored might benefit from a postponement of harvest to maximize output and facilitate handling. Farmers must weigh their harvest's intended use and destination while balancing freshness and practical storage requirements.

Market dynamics, including consumer demand, pricing patterns, and market conditions, significantly influence harvest timing. To maximize returns on investment, farmers must align their harvests with market expectations. Seasons of high demand for harvesting can lead to higher pricing and increased marketability. Conversely, misjudging market trends or overharvesting can result in low pricing and excess supply. Successful market-oriented harvest planning requires access to current market knowledge, understanding customer preferences, and strong relationships with distributors and merchants. Farmers can make strategic decisions about when to harvest by considering these factors.

When it comes to choosing the ideal time to harvest, different crops provide different difficulties and factors to take into account. Harvesting fruits and vegetables at optimal maturity ensures maximum flavor and nutritional value. Delays can result in spoiling and overripening; thus, timing is essential. Harvesting crops like maize and soybeans at the ideal moisture content is to stop post-harvest problems like mold formation. When root crops, like potatoes and carrots, reach a perfect size that strikes a balance between texture and sweetness, they are usually harvested. A comprehensive comprehension of the growth patterns, maturation markers, and vulnerability to environmental stressors of individual crops is necessary.

Technological developments have brought precision agriculture technologies that help farmers make data-driven decisions about when to harvest. Farmers can discover regions of stress or possible illness by using real-time information about crop health provided by remote sensing technologies like drones and satellite photos. Soil moisture levels can be measured by sensors buried in the ground, enabling farmers to manage crop health and irrigation techniques better. By improving our understanding of the variables that affect when to harvest, these tools help farmers make well-informed decisions that maximize output and reduce losses.

The timing of the harvest is heavily influenced by labor availability. Organizing labor during harvest season is essential for crops that need to be harvested by hand, including fruits and vegetables. Farmers must balance the efficiency and availability of labor and the requirement for timely harvesting. Crop readiness and labor capacity may not match due to harvesting delays, which could result in losses from overripening or insufficient workforce. Optimizing the labor aspect in the harvest decision-making process requires organizing and coordinating with seasonal laborers or putting mechanical harvesting solutions into place.

The principles of sustainable agriculture prioritize long-term planning and ecological balance, acknowledging that the well-being of the entire agricultural environment is linked to the optimal period for harvesting. The fertility and health of the soil are enhanced by crop rotation, cover crops, and soil conservation techniques, all of which impact the success of subsequent harvests. By implementing sustainable techniques, agriculture's adverse environmental effects are lessened, and the land is kept productive for future generations. The focus on sustainable agriculture aligns with the overarching objective of feeding an expanding world population while protecting the environment.

In summary, choosing when to harvest is a complex

process that requires a deep comprehension of plant physiology, environmental variables, market dynamics, and technology developments. The delicate balance between plant maturation, meteorological circumstances, and post-harvest factors influences crop quality, production, and marketability. Farmers operate in a challenging environment where timing decisions directly impact agricultural methods' sustainability and financial success. As agriculture develops, the art and science of figuring out when to harvest will become further refined through technology, sustainable practices, and market-oriented tactics.

Proper Harvesting Techniques

An essential part of the agricultural cycle, proper harvesting procedures signal the end of devoted growing efforts and have a bearing on crops' final quality and production. To guarantee that crops are in the best possible condition for market distribution or storage, harvesting is an art that requires a precise balancing act between timing, techniques, and tools. We shall examine the fundamentals of suitable harvesting methods in this section and the behaviors, instruments, and factors that lead to productive harvests in diverse agricultural contexts.

Knowing when a plant will reach maturity is the first step in harvesting a plant correctly. Different crops grow in different ways, and getting the appropriate harvesting time is essential to getting the desired quality and yield. Reliable markers of maturity for fruits and vegetables, such as tomatoes and apples, include color changes, texture, and sugar content. Conversely, cereals such as wheat or rice need close attention to the color and firmness of the kernels. A thorough understanding of plant physiology and consistent crop development monitoring allows farmers to determine the ideal harvesting time. Delays can cause overripening, shortened shelf life, and possible losses, while early harvesting might provide undeveloped crops with lower nutritional value.

The state of the weather dramatically influences the timing of the harvest. Most crops do best in dry, sunny weather because it reduces the chance of soil compaction and makes machinery operation easier. On the other side, excessive rain can muddy fields and cause harvesting to be delayed, especially for crops like grains that need mechanical equipment. Some crops are seriously threatened by frost, so harvesting them early is essential to prevent harm. Farmers who live in areas where weather patterns are erratic need to exercise caution and modify their harvesting times to reduce potential risks. Farmers can better plan their harvests and reduce weather-related losses with contemporary weather-predicting technologies.

Harvesting has changed due to agricultural technology, which offers efficiency and accuracy that traditional techniques frequently need to catch up on. Utilizing specialized machinery, such as fruit-picking machines for orchards or combine harvesters for grains, is known as mechanical harvesting. These devices are made to optimize the harvesting procedure, increasing efficiency and lowering labor costs. Even while mechanical harvesting is effective, it must be calibrated carefully to reduce crop damage and guarantee maximum yields. Maximizing the advantages of mechanical harvesting requires regular maintenance, adjustments, and compliance with manufacturer specifications.

Manual harvesting is still a common and labor-intensive practice in circumstances where mechanized technologies might not be appropriate or economical. Hand harvesting is frequently used for produce that needs to be handled carefully, such as fruits and vegetables. Farmworkers' expertise is crucial when harvesting crops by hand because ineffective methods might cause crop contamination, damage, or bruising. Successful manual harvesting operations depend on worker cooperation, ergonomic instruments, and proper training. Even while manual techniques aren't as quick as their mechanical counterparts, they provide the accuracy and flexibility necessary for some crops and terrain.

Correct harvesting methods are essential not just in the fields but also in the post-harvest processing stage. After harvesting, crops require rapid processing and cautious management to maintain their quality and shelf life. For some fruits and vegetables, quick cooling is essential to halting the ripening process and preserving freshness. Grain must be dried to a specific moisture content to stop mold from growing while it is stored. Harvested crop quality is maintained by appropriate transportation, storage, and packaging practices. Post-harvest management procedures are essential to reducing losses and guaranteeing that crops are in prime condition when consumed.

Harvesting a crop selectively means taking only the ripe or mature parts and letting the remaining portions continue growing. This method benefits crops with asynchronous maturation, in which individual fruits or grains on a plant do not ripen simultaneously. Farmers can increase total production while guaranteeing that every harvested unit satisfies quality criteria using selective harvesting. Finding the crop's ready-to-harvest parts needs continuous monitoring and a thorough grasp of its growth patterns. Selective harvesting is a desirable approach for certain crops, even though it may take longer than harvesting entire fields at once due to the benefits of enhanced quality and increased overall yield.

Throughout the harvesting process, there must be constant observation and evaluation to guarantee the quality of the crops that are produced. Visual inspections, sample testing, and the analysis of chemical compositions using technologies like near-infrared spectroscopy are a few examples of quality control methods. Farmers can detect problems like infections, pest damage, or physiological disorders early in the harvest by implementing strict quality control. This allows farmers to make timely adjustments to farming operations or storage techniques. The integrity of crops is protected from the farm to the market by quality assurance standards covering handling and transporting crops after harvest.

In many farming communities, customary and cultural customs heavily influence harvesting schedules and techniques. Indigenous knowledge passed down through the years frequently includes seasonal indicators, local weather patterns, and observations of nature. Harvesting customs and celebrations rooted in the community may correspond with particular phases of crop growth, demonstrating the close relationship between farming and cultural identity. A healthy relationship between communities and their agricultural landscapes can be fostered by incorporating traditional wisdom with modern farming practices to improve the resilience and sustainability of harvesting processes.

Even with improved harvesting methods, issues still need to be solved by the agricultural industry. There are persistent issues, such as a lack of labor, the high cost of machinery, and the environmental effects of some methods. Reassessing harvesting methods is also necessary in light of the worldwide movement toward sustainable agriculture to reduce ecological footprints. Artificial intelligence, drones, and sensors are examples of precision agriculture technology that can further improve harvesting procedures. Farmers can now collect real-time data on crop health, field conditions, and environmental factors, enabling them to make more informed decisions to enhance sustainability and efficiency.

In summary, effective harvesting methods significantly impact crop quality, productivity, and sustainability, making them essential to thriving agriculture. Farmers negotiate a challenging terrain to guarantee a plentiful crop, from comprehending plant maturity and climatic factors to implementing mechanical or manual harvesting techniques. Maintaining the integrity of crops requires careful attention to handling, processing, and quality control procedures throughout the post-harvest stage. A comprehensive strategy that blends conventional knowledge with modern technology is essential for optimizing harvesting techniques and addressing the issues of a dynamic and interconnected global food chain as agriculture continues to change.

Drying and Curing for Optimal Quality

The quality and durability of crops are established during the sensitive and crucial post-harvest agricultural production stage. Drying and curing are two of the most essential post-harvest procedures that greatly influence farm products' overall flavor, quality, and storage capacity. This section delves into the complex science and art of drying and curing, illuminating the concepts, procedures, and significance of these procedures in maintaining the value of harvested crops.

An age-old technique for agricultural preservation that dates back to ancient civilizations is drying. Drying is mainly done to remove the moisture from harvested crops to stop microbes from growing and spoiling them. In addition to extending the shelf life of crops, this decrease in moisture concentrates tastes and maintains nutritional content. To get the best results, the drying process requires meticulous control over variables, including temperature, humidity, and air circulation.

One of the earliest and most basic techniques for drying crops is sun drying, which uses the sun's inherent energy. This conventional method involves laying out crops in thin layers on level surfaces, leaving them in the sun, and rotating them frequently to guarantee even drying. It works exceptionally well for sun-dried fruits, vegetables, and herbs. Despite being economical and energy-efficient, weather-related factors often constrain its use. Sun drying is still a practical and sustainable solution in areas with steady sunshine and low humidity.

Technological advancements have led to the widespread use of mechanical drying techniques, which provide exact control over the drying environment. Heat is frequently used to speed up the drying process by using infrared radiation or hot air convection. Various crops can be dried effectively and precisely with the help of mechanical dryers, which range in complexity from essential batch dryers to intricate continuous-flow systems. These techniques benefit crops like grains, nuts, and seeds, where uniform drying is critical to halting the formation of mold and preserving quality. Crops are dried quickly and uniformly when temperature and airflow can be controlled, reducing the chance of spoiling.

A specific type of drying called dehydrating entails eliminating moisture from crops so that spoiling is practically nonexistent. Fruits, vegetables, and herbs are frequently processed using this method to create goods like raisins, dried herbs, and dried fruits. Dehydration can be accomplished by mechanical, sun, or air drying. The end products are longer-lasting and lighter yet include much of their original flavor and nutrients. The usefulness of this preservation method is highlighted by the popularity of dehydrated snacks and components in the food business.

Curing is a post-harvest technique wherein some crops are allowed to undergo regulated oxidative or fermentation changes to acquire unique flavors, scents, and textures. Often connected to tobacco, tea, and some fruits, curing is a process that deepens the end product's sensory qualities. For instance, fermentation is used to cure tobacco leaves, creating distinctive scents and smells that add to the varied characteristics of tobacco products. Similarly, tea leaves undergo curing procedures like fermentation or oxidation to develop several kinds of tea, each with a distinct flavor.

A particular kind of curing called fermentation creates new flavors, scents, and textures by breaking down complex chemicals in crops enzymatically. This method frequently produces fermented goods, including chocolate, coffee, and fruit. For example, fermentation breaks down the mucilage layers surrounding coffee beans, affecting the coffee's ultimate flavor. Similarly, the rich and diverse flavor profiles of high-quality chocolate are developed through the fermentation of cocoa beans. To get the intended results, fermentation is a regulated process that must be closely observed.

Oxidation of tea leaves occurs during the curing process, which is an essential stage in the creation of black and oolong tea, among other tea varieties. When tea leaves are exposed to oxygen, enzymatic processes change the chemical makeup of the leaves. This process is known as oxidation. The type of tea produced depends on the oxidation level, which can range from fully oxidized black tea to slightly oxidized oolong tea. The curing procedure improves the tea's flavor, color, and scent, producing various goods to suit consumer tastes.

Although preservation is frequently the primary goal of curing, there are other advantages besides extended shelf life. Fermentation and oxidation are two examples of curing techniques that affect a crop's nutritional value in addition to helping it acquire flavor. For instance, foods that have undergone fermentation frequently have higher nutritional bioavailability and probiotic content, which can improve gut health. Agricultural products get value from the transforming curing process because it gives them distinctive qualities that appeal to customers.

Artisanal curing methods that combine cutting-edge techniques with time-honored processes have seen a rise in popularity in recent years. Artisanal curing often entails small-scale, manual methods that put quality before quantity. Experimentation with various flavors and textures is made possible by emphasizing craftsmanship and attention to detail, which produces distinctive and superior products. This trend aligns with the increasing demand from consumers for handcrafted, locally sourced products that highlight the unique terroir and artisanal skill.

There are many obstacles and factors to consider, even though drying and curing are essential to maintaining and improving the quality of crops. Climate fluctuation concerns reliable and effective drying, especially when sun drying is the primary method. Careful supervision is necessary for mechanical dryers to avoid overheating and preserve product quality. Furthermore, the possibility of contamination or spoiling during the drying and curing process emphasizes the importance of maintaining hygienic conditions. A persistent problem that calls for creative solutions is striking a balance between the need for efficiency and scale and artisanal and traditional methods.

To sum up, drying and curing are essential in the post-harvest handling of agricultural goods. These methods—sun, mechanical, dehydrating, fermenting, or oxidation—are necessary to maintain crops, bring out their flavors, and produce unique goods. These post-harvest practices are successful because they carefully balance environmental factors, technical improvements, and traditional wisdom. The art and science of drying and curing remain crucial in influencing the agricultural processing landscape and guaranteeing the availability of tasty and nutritious crops for customers globally as the demand for high-quality, diverse, and sustainable food items rises.

CHAPTER IX

Post-Harvest Processing

Trimming and Manicuring Buds

In the realm of cannabis farming, trimming, and grooming buds is an essential step that turns unprocessed harvests into finished goods that are ready for the market. Trimming is carefully removing extra leaves and stems from cannabis buds, whereas manicuring concentrates on improving the final product's appearance and potency. This section delves into the art and science of trimming and manicures, illuminating the methods, equipment, and importance of these procedures in the cannabis business.

Removing undesired plant material, mostly leaves and stems, from the harvested cannabis buds is a delicate and exact process known as trimming. The aim is to enhance the finished product's overall potency, quality, and attractiveness. Extra leaves don't add much to the buds' potency and can give off an unwanted flavor when smoked, especially if they lack trichomes, which are resin glands that carry THC. Not only does trimming improve the buds' appearance, but it also makes smoking more enjoyable for users.

Trimming must be done at the right time, usually soon after the cannabis plants have been harvested. It's common to refer to recently harvested cannabis as "wet" or "uncured," and cutting the plant material at this time makes it easier to work with the stuff. The procedure requires close attention to detail since every cut impacts the buds' final appearance and quality. Maintaining the integrity of the buds while eliminating superfluous foliage is a delicate balance that trimmers need to make.

Hand trimming, sometimes called "hand manicuring," is a detailed and time-consuming procedure in which knowledgeable trimmers meticulously cut out undesired plant material from each bud using scissors or pruning shears. Expert trimmers may precisely and individually customize this artisanal method by trimming each bud according to its qualities. Because hand trimming can retain the trichomes and the overall quality of the buds, it is frequently preferred.

In addition to eliminating extra plant material by hand, hand trimming involves precisely sculpting and contouring each bud. Trimmers pay special attention to the buds' structure to guarantee a consistent look and ideal density. This practical method calls for steady hands, an acute eye, and knowledge of the precise attributes that the finished object should have. Although hand trimming requires a lot of time and resources, many cannabis enthusiasts like the artistry and precision it adds to the final buds.

With the evolution of cannabis growing, machine trimming has surfaced as a scalable and efficient alternative to hand trimming, particularly for large-scale operations. Machine trimmers delicately remove extra leaves off buds using automated equipment with revolving blades or tumblers. Although machine trimming is more economical and quicker than hand trimming, it lacks the delicate touch. The trichomes and general quality of the buds may be jeopardized when the blades cut through more than just the leaves.

Machine trimming is efficient, but it has its drawbacks. The final product's consistency may differ, and some contend that the procedure may make each bud seem less distinctive by making it appear more uniform. Furthermore, the visual profile of machine-trimmed buds may differ from that of hand-trimmed buds, which could impact their marketability. The extent of cultivation, the required level of artistry, and consumer preferences often influence the decision between hand and machine trimming.

A manicure concentrates on improving the visual appeal and potency of cannabis buds, going beyond simple cutting. While pruning mainly entails removing extra leaves and stems, manicuring takes further measures to clean and shape the buds, resulting in an aesthetically pleasing and commercially viable product.

One part of manicures is removing "sugar leaves," which are the little leaves that round the buds and are coated in glue. Although sugar leaves are likewise made of cannabinoids, their potency is usually lower than more giant fan leaves. Trimmers carefully trim these sugar leaves to accentuate the buds' structure and enhance their overall beauty. Finding the ideal balance is crucial since too much removal can lessen the final product's efficacy.

Curing is the most critical process after pruning and manicuring the buds. Curing enables the full range of tastes, smells, and potency to develop in the cannabis buds through a long and regulated drying process. The clipped buds are placed in a controlled environment with precise humidity and temperature settings to cure. The gradual drying process improves the whole smoking experience and enhances the terpene profile, adding to the buds' flavor and aroma.

Achieving the best results necessitates proper curing, which takes time and careful attention to detail. Buds are usually kept in jars or other airtight containers that let moisture escape gradually and keep mold or mildew from growing. With the containers periodically opened to allow air exchange, the curing process can take several weeks. As a result, the product is well-cured and has a well-rounded flavor profile, smoother smoke, and increased power.

In addition to being aesthetically pleasing, trimming and manicures must satisfy the high requirements of the cannabis industry. Cannabis goods must adhere to strict rules regarding their safety, strength, and appearance in areas where it is legal. To ensure that cannabis buds match these requirements and are appealing to customers in a crowded market, proper trimming and manicures are essential.

Visual inspections, potency testing, and contamination monitoring for mold and pesticides are examples of quality control methods. In addition to being required by law, upholding these standards is crucial for gaining customers' trust. In the cannabis industry, well-groomed buds that meet or surpass consumer expectations have a higher chance of earning favorable evaluations and building a solid reputation.

Extracts and Concentrates

Extracts and concentrates have become revolutionary products that highlight the plant's adaptability and potency in the ever-changing cannabis consumption scene. These concentrated cannabis products, which range from tinctures and oils to waxes and shatters, give users effective and different ways to enjoy the medical and recreational properties of the plant. This section explores the complex world of cannabis concentrates and extracts, including extraction techniques, various product varieties, consumption patterns, and the products' increasing importance in the cannabis market.

Specialized extraction techniques are used to separate and concentrate the active ingredients in cannabis, including terpenes and cannabinoids, to create extracts and concentrates. Tetrahydrocannabinol (THC) and cannabidiol (CBD) are the principal cannabinoids of interest; each has a distinct effect and possible medicinal uses. To fully use the wealth of cannabinoids found in cannabis plants, a variety of extraction processes are used. Some of the more popular ones are solvent extraction, CO_2 extraction, and rosin pressing.

One of the earliest and most popular techniques for producing cannabis concentrates is solvent extraction. Ethanol, butane, and propane are common solvents chosen for their capacity to dissolve and extract terpenes and cannabinoids from plant material. The procedure yields a solution high in cannabinoids by soaking or washing the cannabis plant material in the selected solvent. A concentrated cannabis extract is left behind once the solvent evaporates.

Even though solvent extraction is practical and flexible, it needs to be carefully post-processed to make sure that any remaining solvents—which could be dangerous if consumed—are removed. Products with distinct consistencies and cannabis profiles, like hash oil, shatter, and wax, are produced using this technique on a large scale.

Carbon dioxide (CO2) extraction has gained popularity due to its accuracy and capacity to yield pure, high-quality extracts. Using this technique, terpenes and cannabinoids are extracted from the cannabis plant using pressurized CO2 as a solvent. Because CO2 extraction has adjustable settings, producers can target particular terpenes and cannabinoids without removing unwanted substances.

Since CO2 extraction does not leave any residual solvents behind, it is considered a safer and more regulated approach than solvent extraction. The end products, like distillate or CO2 oil, are frequently utilized in edibles, tinctures, and vape cartridges because of their consistency and purity in terms of marijuana concentration.

The process of rosin pressing, a solventless extraction technique, releases the cannabinoids and terpenes from cannabis flower or hash by applying pressure and heat. This method, frequently carried out with a hydraulic press, produces rosin, a sticky material. Rosin is a desirable alternative for people looking for a concentrate without solvents because it maintains the entire spectrum of terpenes and cannabinoids without needing them.

Rosin pressing is becoming more and more popular among cannabis fans who prefer the do-it-yourself method due to its ease of use and accessibility. People can make modest rosin at home with a press and heat plates, guaranteeing a potent and pure cannabis concentrate.

A wide range of products are available in the cannabis extracts and concentrates market, and each one is unique in terms of consistency, cannabinoid profile, and mode of consumption. The most popular product categories include shatters, oils, tinctures, waxes, and crystalline isolates.

THC oils and tinctures are a flexible and easily obtained class of extracts with multiple applications. Dropper bottles are commonly used for these liquid concentrates, enabling users to measure and regulate their dosage precisely precisely. While tinctures can be discreetly consumed by adding them to food or beverages, oils are frequently administered sublingually for a quick beginning of action. Oils and tinctures are popular with medicinal and recreational consumers because of their versatility.

The concentrates that have solid or semi-solid consistencies include waxes and shatters. The texture of waxes is softer and more pliable; they resemble beeswax in substance. In contrast, shatters are brittle and unyielding, frequently shattering into "shards" when handled. Both products use different extraction techniques, such as CO2 or butane extraction.

Waxes and shatters are ideal for vaping due to their consistency; vape pens or specialty dab rigs are frequently used. Users can consume cannabis effectively and precisely with vaporization, which also reduces their exposure to combustion byproducts while providing solid effects.

The purest form of cannabinoids is represented by crystalline isolates, frequently isolated to 99% or greater concentrations. Customers can experience THC or CBD without the presence of additional components found in the cannabis plant thanks to this crystalline form that contains only these two cannabinoids. For quick and powerful results, crystalline isolates can be rubbed on or added to food or drinks.

The industry's pursuit of cannabinoid purity is shown in the creation of crystalline isolates, which enable users to customize their cannabis consumption precisely. These isolates provide a distinctive alternative for individuals looking for specific benefits without the unpredictability associated with whole-plant extracts, even while they lack the entourage effect of mixing different cannabinoids and terpenes.

The quest for discrete and effective ingestion techniques, together with a growing understanding of the therapeutic potential of cannabinoids and altering consumer preferences, have all contributed to the rising popularity of cannabis extracts and concentrates. Vaporization has mainly gained popularity among users as a smokeless substitute that offers a quick start of effects.

Vape cartridges with cannabis oil or distillate within have become very popular due to their discreetness and ease of use. These cartridges give consumers a convenient and portable way to consume cannabis extracts because they work with vape pens and vaporizer batteries. Vape cartridges are a popular option for both inexperienced and seasoned cannabis users due to their controlled dosage and slight vaporization-related smell.

By utilizing a dab rig or specialized vaporizer, dabbers vape cannabis concentrates, usually oils, shatters, or waxes. With a quick onset and strong effects, this approach provides a highly effective way to take pure cannabis. Dabbing enthusiasts enjoy that they may customize their experience by selecting from a range of concentrates that have varying profiles of cannabinoids.

Storage and Preservation

The significance of storage and preservation in agriculture cannot be emphasized. After crops are harvested, their journey doesn't end; instead, it moves into a critical stage where the objective is to preserve nutritional content, freshness, and quality. Produce storage and preservation are essential for satisfying the needs of an expanding global population, minimizing waste, and guaranteeing food security. This section explores the different approaches, tools, and factors that go into preserving agricultural wealth by delving into the complex world of storage and preservation.

Traditional storage techniques have been crucial for maintaining a consistent food supply throughout history and protecting crops. People have stored fruits, vegetables, and tubers in root cellars for ages. These subterranean buildings offer a chilly, dark, and humid atmosphere that slows ripening and prolongs the produce's shelf life. In areas with plenty of sunlight, sun-drying has also been a standard method of preserving fruits, vegetables, and grains. The technique is to spread the crops in thin layers and let the sun naturally dry them off.

Natural preservatives like salt, sugar, and vinegar are another age-old technique. These compounds aid in food preservation by preventing the growth of bacteria that cause spoiling. An old method called fermentation uses beneficial bacteria to break down the sugars and starches in crops, resulting in an acidic environment that inhibits the growth of pathogenic microorganisms. Customary preservation techniques, derived from indigenous knowledge and customized to local circumstances, demonstrate societies' ingenuity in guaranteeing a dependable provision of food.

More complex storage techniques were required as agriculture developed to handle greater produce yields and maintain freshness for extended periods. Cold storage has emerged as a game-changer with its innovative use of temperature control to impede the physiological processes that cause spoiling. Modern cold storage facilities must include refrigeration and freezing to maintain the quality and nutritional content of perishable foods like fruits and vegetables.

Refrigeration slows down the rate of ripening and lowers microbial activity by keeping temperatures above freezing. Fruits, vegetables, dairy products, and other perishables are frequently used with it. In contrast, freezing entails bringing the temperature below the freezing point, stopping the microbiological and enzymatic processes that cause spoiling. Fruits, vegetables, meats, and prepared foods are frequently kept in frozen storage because they extend their shelf life while maintaining their nutritional value.

From the farm gate to the consumer, cold storage plays a crucial role in the supply chain by preserving seasonal crops and lowering the need for imported items during off-seasons. With the introduction of controlled environment storage, cold storage was further improved by modifying humidity, carbon dioxide, and oxygen levels to establish ideal conditions for particular types of produce, maintaining quality and prolonging shelf life.

Food preservation using sealed containers, or canning, has been a centuries-old culinary practice. To prevent rotting and ensure long-term preservation, this approach involves heat-processing food in jars to eliminate or inactivate microorganisms. This method is especially well-liked for fruits, vegetables, pickled goods, jams, and sauces. Food can be preserved by keeping flavors and nutrients through canning.

With the invention of home canning, households could now enjoy a broader range of foods outside of the growing season and preserve the bounty of their harvests. Commercially canned goods are now widely available, providing consumers with a dependable and easy way to obtain preserved meals. To establish an environment unfavorable to spoilage bacteria, canning requires exact processing durations, careful attention to hygiene, and the use of the right amounts of acid.

Traditional food preservation techniques like dehydration and drying involve removing moisture to prevent microorganisms from growing. Standard methods to lower the water content of fruits, vegetables, herbs, and meats include sun drying, air drying, or utilizing specialized dehydrators. Food is preserved by this procedure, which also concentrates flavors, making dried goods useful in various culinary applications.

For example, dried fruits make a convenient and wholesome snack, and dried herbs give food a pungent taste. You may rehydrate dehydrated veggies for casseroles, stews, and soups. The dehydration process prolongs the shelf life of items by preventing enzymatic processes that lead to deterioration. Dehydrated meals are also convenient for storing and traveling because they are small and light.

A contemporary preservation method called vacuum sealing first eliminates air from a pouch or container before sealing it. Vacuum sealing reduces the amount of oxygen in the air, which slows down oxidation and microbiological development that cause food to deteriorate. This technique applies to perishable goods like cheeses, meats, and prepared foods.

Foods kept in a refrigerator or freezer can retain their freshness for longer thanks to vacuum-sealed packaging. Additionally, the lack of oxygen keeps the freezer burn at bay and preserves the quality of frozen foods. This method enables practical and space-saving storage and is used in consumer vacuum-sealing devices and professional food packing.

A contentious component of food preservation is chemical preservatives, as there are worries about potential health effects and a desire for more natural alternatives. Chemical preservatives like sulfur dioxide, sorbic acid, and sodium benzoate are added to various food items to stop bacteria, yeasts, and molds from growing. These chemicals frequently preserve baked goods, drinks, and processed meals.

CHAPTER X

Troubleshooting Common Issues

Addressing Nutrient Deficiencies

Plant growth, production, and general vigor are all negatively impacted by nutrient shortages, which present a severe threat to plant health and productivity. Nutrients are vital to many biochemical reactions and are necessary for the plant to perform basic tasks, including photosynthesis, cell division, and energy transmission. Thriving agriculture and horticulture depend critically on identifying and correcting nutrient shortages, which calls for a sophisticated knowledge of plant physiology, soil dynamics, and nutrient interactions.

Various macro- and micronutrients are necessary for the healthy growth of plants. While micronutrients like iron (Fe), manganese (Mn), zinc (Zn), copper (Cu), molybdenum (Mo), and boron (B) are necessary for trace levels, macronutrients like nitrogen (N), phosphorus (P), potassium (K), calcium (Ca), magnesium (Mg), and sulfur (S) are needed in more significant numbers. Visible symptoms may indicate imbalances or shortages in these nutrients, offering essential hints for diagnosis and treatment.

Lack of nitrogen is one of the most frequent nutritional problems in plants. Nitrogen-deficient plants frequently show stunted development, chlorosis (leaf yellowing), and an overall lack of vigor. Older leaves are more conspicuously deficient as nitrogen is movable within the plant and prefers to migrate to a newer development. Fermentation must provide more nitrogen to address the nitrogen deficit, guaranteeing a balanced nutrient intake to promote healthy plant development.

Lack of phosphorus is another common issue in farming. Energy transmission, root growth, and flowering all depend on phosphorus. Phosphorus-deficient plants may grow slowly, mature later, and have discolored leaves and a purplish color. Phosphorus-rich fertilizers or amendments are frequently used to remedy this shortage, encouraging better nutrient uptake and utilization by the plant.

An essential macronutrient for general plant health is potassium. Potassium-deficient plants can show signs including yellowing of the leaves, burned leaf margins and heightened vulnerability to illnesses and environmental stressors. Applying fertilizers containing potassium is necessary to address potassium deficiencies, highlighting the significance of preserving a balanced nutrient profile to promote ideal plant growth.

Calcium and magnesium deficiency are frequently related and affect different aspects of plant physiology. Meanwhile, interveinal chlorosis is a sign of magnesium insufficiency and deformed or necrotic leaf margins can result from calcium deficiency. Calcium insufficiencies can be remedied by applying gypsum or lime, while magnesium can be obtained using fertilizers that include magnesium compounds.

Though less prevalent, sulfur shortage can cause younger leaves to become yellow. The synthesis of amino acids and overall plant metabolism depend heavily on sulfur. Sulfur deficits are addressed by elemental sulfur or fertilizers containing sulfate, which guarantees a complete nutrient supply for healthy plant growth.

Because micronutrients are required in trace levels, deficits in them pose particular issues. For example, a lack of iron causes interveinal chlorosis, which affects the plant's capacity to perform photosynthesis and has prominent green veins. Iron chelates applied topically or in the soil are popular methods for treating iron deficiency. Comparably, low manganese causes chlorosis, frequently seen in younger leaves. Applications of manganese sulfate can help this shortage and encourage strong plant development.

Leaf deformities and reduced growth, especially in the new growth, are signs of zinc deficiency. Enzyme activation and general plant metabolic activities depend on zinc. Applying zinc-containing fertilizers through foliar sprays or soil amendments is one way to address zinc deficiency.

Even though it is uncommon, a copper shortage can cause withering and deformed growth. Copper is essential for several plant enzymatic reactions, and deficits can be addressed by fungicides or fertilizers containing copper. Conversely, lacking molybdenum interferes with nitrogen metabolism and causes symptoms like leaf cupping and yellowing. Sodium molybdate is a standard molybdenum used to supplement people who are deficient in this mineral.

Although less common, a lack of boiron can have a significant impact on the growth of plants. Boron-deficient plants can grow erratically, have fragile leaves, and develop poorly in flowers or fruits. Fertilizers and soil amendments containing boron must mitigate boron deficits and ensure adequate pollination and seed development.

A thorough knowledge of plant symptoms and a systematic approach to eliminating potential causes are essential for diagnosing nutrient deficiency. Plant tissue analysis, soil tests, and visual symptoms are valuable for determining deficiencies and creating focused corrective actions. The acidity or alkalinity of the soil affects whether nutrients are more or less accessible to plants, which in turn affects the pH levels of the soil.

Plant health can also be impacted by nutritional imbalances in addition to deficits. Nutrient toxicity can result from overfertilization or unbalanced nutrient ratios, which can upset plant physiology and worsen nutrient deficits. Promoting optimal plant health and reducing nutrient-related problems requires balancing giving plants enough nutrients and avoiding overfertilization.

Crop rotation, cover crops, and the addition of organic matter are examples of cultivation techniques that improve soil health and nutrient availability. Fertilized soils that are well-structured and have a diverse microbial population help plants absorb and cycle nutrients more effectively. Precision and organic farming are examples of sustainable agriculture techniques that reduce nutrient losses and encourage a nutrient-balanced ecosystem.

In summary, treating nutrient deficiencies is essential to growing effective plants and calls for a comprehensive grasp of nutrient interactions, soil properties, and plant physiology. For optimum plant health and maximum crop yields, timely diagnosis and focused remedial actions—whether via foliar or soil amendments—are essential. Farmers and cultivators must adopt a proactive approach to nutrient management and understand the complex interactions between plants, soil, and nutrients to promote sustainable and fruitful agricultural systems. We open the door to a future of robust crops, abundant harvests, and sustainable agriculture by becoming experts at correcting nutritional deficits.

Dealing with Environmental Stress

Plant life faces a significant challenge from environmental stress, which affects growth, development, and total output. Plants are subjected to an increasing number of stresses due to climate change, such as severe temperatures, droughts, flooding, salt, and pollution. Sustainable agriculture and ecosystem health must adapt to these environmental challenges. This section investigates the different types of environmental stress, how they affect plants, and how to improve resilience so that our green friends can continue to thrive.

Extremes of temperature are one of the most common types of environmental stress. There are ideal temperature ranges for plant growth, and changes can significantly impact these ranges. Heat stress from high temperatures can damage cellular structures, interfere with photosynthesis, and change metabolic processes. On the other hand, low temperatures can cause chilling injury, compromising the integrity of cell membranes and enzyme activity. To adapt to temperature stress, plants produce heat shock proteins and modify the fluidity of their membranes, among other strategies. One of the most critical tactics for reducing the effects of temperature stress is climate-resilient plant breeding, which aims to create cultivars tolerant of severe temperatures.

Drought stress is a widespread environmental problem that has far-reaching effects on ecosystems and agriculture. Lack of water interferes with a plant's ability to perform its regular tasks, which reduces photosynthesis, causes wilting, and eventually hinders growth. In response to drought stress, plants build deeper root systems, produce osmoprotectants, and close their stomata to minimize water loss. To manage and adapt to water scarcity and ensure sustainable water usage in agriculture, three essential measures include developing drought-tolerant crop types, rainwater gathering, and precision irrigation.

Another type of environmental stress is flooding, which is more common in low-lying places or locations that frequently see severe rains. Plant roots receive less oxygen from soggy soils, which impedes their ability to absorb nutrients and perform metabolic functions. Plants respond to flooding by forming aerenchymas and changing the shape of their roots, among other adaptive features. Utilizing cover crops, flood-resistant crop types, and drainage systems are practical ways to lessen the adverse effects of flooding on agricultural productivity and plant health.

Agriculture is seriously threatened by salinity stress, caused by high salt content in the soil or water, particularly in arid and semi-arid areas. Plants' ability to absorb water, maintain ion balance, and absorb nutrients can all be hampered by high salt concentrations. Halophytes, adapted to saline environments, offer critical genetic resources for creating crops that can withstand salt. In addition, water management techniques like drip irrigation and soil supplements like gypsum are crucial for controlling salinity stress and preserving soil health.

Air pollution affects plant health by bringing toxins into the atmosphere through agricultural practices, vehicle exhaust, and industrial emissions. Common air pollutants that can cause plant oxidative stress, resulting in leaf damage and decreased development, include ozone, sulfur dioxide, and nitrogen oxides. Sustainable land-use techniques, using plants to remove environmental pollutants, and phytoremediation all help lessen the adverse effects of air pollution on plant ecosystems.

One type of environmental stress that has severe effects on plants and human health is heavy metal poisoning. Lead, cadmium, and mercury are among the elements that can enter the soil due to mining, industrial operations, and inappropriate waste management. These metals build up in the tissues of plants, interfering with physiological functions and making harvests unfit for human consumption. Remediating contaminated sites may be possible via phytoremediation, which removes heavy metals from soil using plants that accumulate metals. More stringent environmental restrictions and effective waste management are also necessary to stop more heavy metal pollution.

Agriculture and conservation must adopt adaptive techniques because of the increasing frequency and intensity of environmental stressors brought on by global climate change. Changes in temperature regimes, heightened occurrences of extreme weather events, and variations in precipitation patterns provide problems that call for creative solutions. Increasing agricultural systems' resilience to the many effects of climate change is facilitated by agroforestry, crop variety diversification, and incorporating climate-resilient methods.

It is impossible to overstate the importance of plant hormones in mediating reactions to environmental stress. To improve water retention, ABA plays a crucial role in the responses to drought stressors by controlling stomatal closure and modifying gene expression. Another significant plant hormone, ethylene, affects how plants react to different challenges, such as pathogen invasion and flooding. Knowledge of the complex signaling networks controlled by these hormones helps build stress-tolerant crops through genetic engineering and sheds light on the molecular mechanisms behind stress responses.

In addition, the rhizosphere—the area of soil affected by plant roots—is essential to the cycling of nutrients and interactions between plants and microbes. Plants and beneficial soil microorganisms, such as nitrogen-fixing bacteria and mycorrhizal fungi, develop symbiotic interactions that improve plants' resistance to environmental stress. A healthy rhizosphere is fostered by conservation tillage, cover crops, and applying organic amendments, which increases microbial diversity and resilience in agroecosystems.

In summary, combating environmental stress necessitates a multimodal strategy incorporating cutting-edge science, creative technology, and environmentally friendly farming methods. Promoting plant ecosystem resilience becomes essential to guaranteeing food security, biodiversity protection, and ecosystem sustainability as humanity struggles with the effects of climate change. We may overcome the difficulties presented by environmental stress by adopting adaptive techniques, such as genetic engineering and precision irrigation, and raise robust plants that can flourish in a world that is changing quickly. This pledge protects future generations' access to agricultural output and the fragile equilibrium of our world's ecosystems.

Solving Common Growing Problems

Growing plants is a complex process that frequently faces many difficulties, whether in a greenhouse, farm, or backyard garden. Growers fight a never-ending war to maintain the health and vigor of their plants, battling everything from pests and diseases to environmental conditions and nutrient imbalances. This section examines the typical developing issues that arise in agriculture and horticulture, providing various thorough answers to promote good plant growth and insights into the underlying causes of these issues.

For growers, pest infestations pose a constant threat since they can ruin crops and drastically reduce harvests. By consuming plant tissues, spreading disease, or interfering with vital physiological functions, insects, mites, and other pests can harm plants. An all-encompassing strategy to deal with pest-related problems is the emergence of Integrated Pest Management (IPM). This approach combines cultural customs like crop rotation, biological controls like predatory insects and parasitoids, and the prudent application of chemical treatments. Growers can lessen the impact of pests while maintaining ecological balance and using fewer chemical pesticides by implementing an integrated pest management (IPM) strategy.

Diseases are another significant hazard to plant health brought on by various pathogens, including bacteria, viruses, fungi, and nematodes. The symptoms of fungal infections, including rot, spots, and wilting, can be lessened using fungicidal treatments, disease-resistant plant kinds, and good cleanliness. Viral infections frequently call for the removal and killing of afflicted plants to stop the spread of the virus. Still, bacterial diseases may respond better to copper-based sprays or antibiotic treatments. Crop rotations and soil additives like organic matter are used in nematode control to make the environment less friendly to these microscopic pests.

Environmental stressors such as drought, flooding, and extremely high or low temperatures can hinder plant growth and development. Temperature extremes and water scarcity can be lessened using climate-resilient agricultural methods, such as precision irrigation and crop variety selection. For regions that flood frequently, having adequate drainage infrastructure and planting crops resistant to flooding are essential. Growers can adjust their cultivation techniques to provide the best growing circumstances for their plants by knowing the particular environmental stressors in a given area.

Common problems such as nutrient imbalances and deficiencies can negatively impact plant health. Addressing these issues requires an understanding of the nutritional requirements of plants. Growers can evaluate nutrient levels and modify fertilization techniques based on soil testing results. Maintaining nutrient-rich soils is aided by cover crops, organic amendments, and balanced fertilizers. Companion planting involves growing crops that complement one another regarding nutrient requirements and can also help minimize imbalances and improve soil fertility.

In agriculture, weeds are frequently viewed as a nuisance because they compete with crops for nutrients, water, and sunlight. Herbicide use and mechanical techniques like mulching and cultivation are examples of weed management tactics. In addition to offering other advantages like nitrogen fixing and soil erosion prevention, cover crops, and ground coverings are efficient at inhibiting the growth of weeds. Various weed control techniques should be used in conjunction with strategic planning for effective and sustainable weed management.

Plant cultivation performance depends on healthy soil, and its deterioration can cause a wide range of developing issues. Compaction, nitrogen depletion, and soil erosion are frequent problems that jeopardize soil health. Enhancing soil structure, increasing nutrient content, and reducing erosion are some of the benefits of conservation tillage, cover crops, and organic matter assimilation. The health of the soil is given top priority in sustainable farming practices because of its critical role in promoting plant development and ecosystem resilience.

Cultural techniques, such as crop rotation and appropriate spacing, are essential in stopping the spread of pests and diseases. Crop rotation breaks pest and pathogen life cycles, which lowers their frequency in upcoming plantings. Plants spaced appropriately allow air to circulate, which lowers the risk of fungal infections and creates an atmosphere that is less inviting to pests. These straightforward but efficient methods reduce the need for chemical interventions while improving plant health overall.

Adequate water use is essential for farming, and mishandled irrigation techniques can result in several issues. Increased susceptibility to infections, nutrient leaching, and root rot can all be consequences of overwatering. On the other hand, underwatering can cause drought stress and impede the growth of plants. Effective irrigation techniques, such as soaker hoses or drip irrigation, can help keep soil moisture levels constant. Effective water management requires tracking soil moisture, considering plant water requirements, and modifying irrigation techniques as necessary.

A frequent problem is inadequate pollination, especially for fruit and vegetable crops. Many plants depend on pollinators like bees and butterflies for successful reproduction. Reductions in the number of pollinators require deliberate steps to increase pollination. A robust and healthy pollinator community is facilitated by planting various blooming plants, avoiding overusing pesticides, and providing habitat for pollinators. If there aren't enough natural pollinators, growers may consider using hand pollination methods.

Improper pruning and training techniques can impact plant structure, yield, and general health. Pruning aids in controlling the size, form, and fruit output of plants. On the other hand, incorrect pruning can result in decreased yields, disease entrance points, and structural instability. Effective pruning requires knowing the particular crop requirements, appropriate scheduling, and using sharp, sterilized equipment. Training plants encourages healthy growth habits and makes light penetration easier, which maximizes photosynthesis and plant productivity overall—especially in trellised or espaliered systems.

In summary, managing typical growing issues

necessitates a thorough and coordinated strategy considering several elements influencing plant health. Growers must take proactive measures to ensure effective cultivation, from driving pests and diseases to mitigating environmental stress and using appropriate cultural methods. With its focus on soil health, ecological balance, and responsible resource management, sustainable agriculture provides a framework for navigating and reducing the difficulties associated with plant cultivation. Growers who adopt these holistic approaches support the long-term sustainability of our agricultural systems, the environment, and the resilience and productivity of their crops.

CONCLUSION

To sum up, "Marijuana Mastery: Essential Strategies for a Successful Grow" is an all-inclusive manual that provides vital insights into the art and science of marijuana growing for both rookie and seasoned growers. With a wealth of knowledge that enables readers to start successful cannabis production endeavors, the author deftly navigates the challenges of cannabis farming.

The e-book starts by providing a solid foundation by going into great detail on the structure of the plant, its growth stages, and the available strains. After that, it explores the vital elements of fruitful growth, covering essential aspects, including light, soil, nutrients, and water. The author's proficiency is evident as they walk readers through the nuances of giving their plants the best possible setting.

"Marijuana Mastery" stands out because it emphasizes a comprehensive method of growing. Beyond the technical details, the e-book delves into the subtleties of keeping a robust and healthy cannabis garden, including subjects like disease prevention, insect control, and typical problem-solving. The learning process becomes practical when case studies and real-world examples are included.

Additionally, the e-book incorporates the newest developments, innovations, and legal considerations to keep up with the rapidly changing marijuana farming landscape. The techniques provided in the book are flexible and progressive, catering to the needs of all readers, whether their goals are personal use or business exploration. From home growers looking for personal use to entrepreneurs aiming for commercial production, " Marijuana Mastery " has everyone covered.

All things considered, "Marijuana Mastery" proves to be a priceless tool for anyone hoping to become an expert in the growing of cannabis. Its combination of in-depth expertise, helpful guidance, and forward-thinking perspectives establishes it as a go-to manual for individuals dedicated to succeeding in their marijuana-growing pursuits.

Thank you for buying and reading/listening to our book. If you found this book useful/helpful please take a few minutes and leave a review on the platform where you purchased our book. Your feedback matters greatly to us.

www.ingramcontent.com/pod-product-compliance
Lightning Source LLC
Chambersburg PA
CBHW052050150726
48002CB00002B/823